18

WORSLEY WARDLEY HIGH SCHOOL

Presented to

Fiona Foley

on

9th Nov 1983

for effort

during the School Year

P. F. Byron

Headmaster

PAVLOVA

PAVLOVA

A Collection of Memoirs

Compiled by A.H. Franks

A DA CAPO PAPERBACK

Library of Congress Cataloging in Publication Data

Main entry under title:

Pavlova, a collection of memoirs.

(A Da Capo paperback)
Reprint. Originally published: Pavlova, a biography.
London : Burke, 1956.
Includes index.
1. Pavlova, Anna, 1881-1931. 2. Ballet dancers—
Russian S.F.S.R.—Biography. I. Franks, A.H. (Arthur
Henry), 1907-
GV1785.P3P38 1981 792.8'2'0924 [B] 81-5554
ISBN 0-306-80149-3 AACR2

This Da Capo Press paperback edition of
Pavlova: A Collection of Memoirs
is an unabridged republication of the first
edition entitled *Pavlova: A Biography* published in London in 1956.
It is reprinted by arrangement with
Burke Publishing Co., Ltd.

Published by Da Capo Press, Inc.
A Subsidiary of Plenum Publishing Corporation
233 Spring Street, New York, N.Y. 10013

Manufactured in the United States of America

By A. H. Franks

Girls' Book of Ballet
Twentieth Century Ballet
Ballet: A Decade of Endeavour

Approach to Ballet
Ballet for Film and Television

Contents

Illustrations

ILLUSTRATIONS

INTRODUCTION

The primary function of this book is to commemorate the twenty-fifth anniversary of the death of Anna Pavlova, and to establish a composite but clear picture, both of the ballerina and the woman. It is true that her name remains even today better known than many distinguished dancers who are still alive, and indeed than some who are still dancing; but the extent of her hold over a world-wide public, her ability and the strengths as well as the weaknesses of her personality no longer remain in sharp focus.

Victor Dandré wrote her biography shortly after her death, but as her husband he naturally and understandably coloured his narrative, so that it was noted more for its adulation than its insight into her character. Valerian Svetlov, on the other hand, wrote a magnificent work on her, but this was never translated into English; and now it seems unobtainable even in France. Others too have written books and monographs; but there has been no recent attempt to develop a three-dimensional picture of this fabulous creature.

Each one among the contributors has written about diverse aspects and qualities of her life. Some over a period of years developed firm friendships, others knew her professionally, and yet others met her but once or twice. My own short biographical sketch springs from yet another standpoint, for in addition to the fact that I never met Pavlova I can scarcely claim after seeing but one or two performances to remember her vividly in action. By talking for long hours with many who did know her, by digesting volume after volume of press cuttings and other material, however, I have been able to conjure a detailed picture into my mind's eye.

INTRODUCTION

In the preparation of the book I have enjoyed the constant aid of the small informal committee who have worked in the closest and most enthusiastic co-operation with me. They were all members of Pavlova's company, and travelled the world with her. I owe much gratitude to them—Kathleen Crofton, Rita Glynde, Sylvia Kirkwhite, Cleo Nordi and Joan van Wart—for their lack of cynicism in a cynical world, as well as for their practical assistance.

Various members of the Pavlova Commemoration Committee itself have also been a great help, lending without hesitation precious documents and photographs. Margaret Drew and "Monty" Morris put into my hands invaluable collections of material which to them must be beyond price. Stanley Judson, who toured for some time with the Company, also brought me his entire memorabilia of "Madame," as did Murilova, another of her "girls."

All the contributors have foresworn their fees for the purpose of swelling the fund which is to go towards the several projects the Pavlova Commemoration Committee are presenting for this 25th Anniversary year.

For permission to reprint the fascinating and intimate article by Michel Fokine, which was written shortly after Pavlova's death for a special issue of *Dance Magazine of America*, I am indebted to the publishers and proprietors of that periodical. Similarly, for permission to reproduce once more Pavlova's own "Pages of My Life" translated by Sebastian Voirol, I express my gratitude to Michel de Brunoff of Paris.

RICHMOND, SURREY — A. H. F.
October 1955

Chapter One

A BIOGRAPHICAL SKETCH

A. H. Franks

AMONG all the great dancers who flourished during the first quarter of the twentieth century, very few left any enduring impression on the public memory. Mention of the names of Nijinsky or Pavlova, however, still evokes some response even from those who are not particularly interested in ballet.

Nijinsky's fame is partly attributable to his sensational dancing, partly to the vicissitudes of his private life and partly to the exaggerations of the popular press on both his dancing and his life. Pavlova, on the other hand, although more was written about her in the world press than about any other dancer before or since, was the cause of but few sensations, either concerning her dancing or her private life. Why, then, twenty-five years after her death are so many of us still vividly interested in a life which contains no major scandals and which is marked throughout by that commendable but unexciting quality of unrelenting dedication to her art? Some possess a greatness which can be apprehended only by the comparative few, others a quality which by its simplicity communicates itself to the world. One kind is no better or more elevated than the other, but only different. The art of Charlie Chaplin is no less great through the universality of its appeal; nor that of T. S. Eliot because it belongs only to the minority. Perhaps Pavlova's greatness lay both in simplicity and profundity.

Born prematurely in St. Petersburg in February 1881, she was the only child of her mother's second marriage. So weak and puny was this future ballerina that her parents hastened to have her baptised, a ceremony that was carried out three days after her birth. She was endowed with the name of Anna because of the saint whose feast is celebrated on that day.

For several months thereafter Anna did not stake a particularly strong claim on life, and spent a large part of her time literally wrapped in cotton wool. Gradually the anxiety of her mother decreased, however, as she developed into a normal but by no means robust toddler.

During her early childhood she was often ill, suffering all the usual complaints of infancy, and some others, including measles, scarlet fever, and even diphtheria. All parents are at times quite at a loss to understand how their children survive the many hazards of childhood. Pavlova afforded her mother more than a fair share of shocks and anxieties. Nevertheless, slowly and miraculously she began to take a firmer grip upon life, so that the next event of note came when her mother took an eight-year-old Anna for a Christmas treat to see the Imperial Russian Ballet perform *The Sleeping Beauty*.

Her father died when Anna was two years old and at times her mother was virtually penniless. Pavlova herself in a newspaper article said that often she and her mother had nothing to eat for days on end but rye bread and cabbage soup. As she began to grow up she realised more and more that her mother was denying herself in order to look after her only child. A visit to the ballet, then, must certainly have represented a wonderful treat. In her own words, written of course many years later, she said of that little occasion:

> I was spellbound . . . I gazed and gazed, and wild plans began to circulate in my brain. It was the second act and the *corps de ballet* were waltzing together.
>
> "Nura," said my mother, amazed at my excitement, "wouldn't you like to join these people and dance with them?"
>
> "No," I replied without hesitation, "I would rather dance by myself, like the lovely Sleeping Beauty. One day I will, and in this very theatre."
>
> My mother laughed, but I was lost in my dream and did not heed her. At eight years old I had found the one, the unchanging ambition of my life.

At first her mother hardly listened to the child's entreaties to be permitted to dance. Then she attempted to temporise by promising that when she grew up she should be allowed to go to ballets and parties. But Anna was not to be put off with such superficialities.

> "I do not mean that kind of dancing," I said resolutely. "I want to be a ballet dancer, like Sleeping Beauty."
>
> I had made up my mind; a ballet dancer I would be. But I had little reckoned with the difficulties. First there was the opposition of my mother to overcome; then the director of the academy pronounced me too young and said I must wait another two years. I sighed, but I waited."

At the end of that period, in 1891, the ten-year-old Pavlova, although still frail, had apparently shaken off all the effects of her illnesses, for she passed without difficulty the very strenuous health examination imposed by the academy. She also passed the tests of intelligence and gracefulness.

After which, embracing the situation in her own words: "My toil and my suffering had begun." Discipline and exercises, work and yet more work became not merely the governing factors of Pavlova's life, from that time until her death, but the best part of life itself—just as they are for every dedicated dancer.

Soon, however, Pavlova had become an outstanding student both in the dance and in general education. Before long great ballet teachers whose names are uttered with reverence by the dancers and teachers of today, were prophesying a brilliant future for her. In a little under four years she made her first appearance on stage, in a school performance with Fokine. On this occasion she danced in *La Fille mal Gardée*. Her first public performance at the Maryinsky came shortly after when she appeared as a *coryphée* in *Pas des Aimées* from *La Fille du Pharaon*, at a benefit performance in honour of Christian Johannsen. This début was marked by a little incident which typifies a presence of mind on stage which belongs to all great theatrical artists. During her dance she pirouetted so enthusiastically that she lost control and fell into the prompter's box, collapsing with a bump, her back to the audience. The laughter in no way caused her to lose her presence of mind, for with a smile and a curtsey she made graceful acknowledgment, as though all had been planned and the idea of an accident too remote for consideration.

But the young Pavlova soon began to have her difficulties. Karsavina in *Theatre Street* conjures up in one of her surpassing word pictures the peculiar outlook of a particular epoch and the struggles of an artist to reconcile herself to that outlook:

> Three pupils of great promise were about to finish school this year, Anna Pavlova amongst them. She was

> so frail as to seem, in our opinion, much weaker than the other two. The pupils' undiscerning admiration was all for virtuosity: our ideals shaped after a robust, compact figure of Legnani's type. Pavlova at that time hardly realised that in her lithe shape and in her technical limitations lay the greatest strength of her charming personality. Romanticism was not the fashion any more. The very figure of our dancers, as compared with the silhouette of those of half a century ago, clearly showed the reversion of taste from an idealised vision towards the attractions of more material charm.
>
> In pursuit of contemporary ideals our stage lost sight of what may seem a paradox, but is a truth—that the ends of choreographic beauty are not always best served by perfect physical harmony. Some of Taglioni's most exquisite poses had their origin in the fact that her arms were disproportionately long.
>
> Meagreness being considered an enemy of good looks, the opinion prevailed that Anna Pavlova needed feeding up. She must have thought it, too, as she swallowed conscientiously cod-liver oil, the school doctor's panacea, and the aversion of us all. Like the rest of us, she strove to emulate the paragon of virtuosity, Legnani. Luckily for her, Guerdt fully divined the quality of her talent. It pained him to see executed by the delicate limbs of Pavlova what seemed consistent only with the hard set musculature of the Italian dancer. He advised her not to strive after the effects that seemed to endanger her frail structure.

For her passing out examination in February 1899 she appeared in *The False Dryads*, for which her teacher Guerdt had arranged the choreography, and in a variation from Petipa's *The Vestal Virgin*. Valerian Svetlov in his biography of Pavlova wrote of this occasion:

> It was her first public appearance, and she at once caught the eyes of all. She was delicate, svelte, and pliant like a reed, with the open expression of a little

> Spanish girl; ethereal and fleeting, she was as graceful and fragile as a piece of Sèvres porcelain. But at times she assumed classical poses, and then, clad in a peplum, she recalled some charming Tanagra statuette so vividly that it was really deceptive.
>
> With a delightful childlike simplicity she mimed her flirtation scene with a young peasant boy and danced in the midst of the false Dryads with mischievous impulsive fun. It was young, fresh, enchanting. There were no other words for it, except that in this young girl's mime there was already something which had neither been learnt nor assumed, but which revealed a soul. The variation from *The Vestal Virgin*, which was of greater interest, showed that it did not need a great prophet to foretell a very brilliant future for this young pupil. I forget what marks she was given by the jury, but in my mind I gave her full marks.

At about the same time another dancer described her:

> She was a very thin girl, slightly above average height. A charming smile, and beautiful eyes that were a little sad. Her legs were long, slim, and very beautiful, with an extraordinarily arched instep. Her whole body was graceful, delicate, and ethereal, as if she were trying to leave the earth.

Having graduated from the academy Pavlova developed with speed and certainty, so that soon she began to live more and more in the admiration of a highly discriminating audience. In her very first year with the Imperial Ballet she brought her own particular interpretation to bear on a number of *coryphée* roles. In 1902 she was promoted to the rank of second soloist, in 1903 to first soloist, and in 1905 to ballerina.

In that same year too she danced for the first time *Le Cygne*, more frequently referred to as *The Dying Swan*, the solo specially arranged for her by Fokine, and by which she was

Pavlova the pupil, at the age of twelve

About ten years old, having recently joined the school of the Imperial Russian Ballet

An early portrait, taken in Russia

As Rime in *The Four Seasons* at St. Petersburg, a part she played very early in her career

to become most famous throughout the world for almost her entire career. Undoubtedly it was her immediate success in this small number, her ability so uncannily to interpret the noble creature, first with its seemingly effortless movement and then in the agony of death that encouraged the authorities at the Maryinsky in 1906 to give her the role of Odette Odile in *Le Lac des Cygnes*. Shortly after she became a *prima ballerina*. Three years later, in 1909, she celebrated her tenth anniversary as an artist of the Imperial Theatre, performing the title role in *La Bayadère* to mark the occasion.

After rising to *prima ballerinadom* Pavlova, as was customary for leading artists of Czarist Russia, received frequent leaves of absence during close seasons and made various tours of Europe. The first came in 1907 when with Adolph Bohm she visited Stockholm, Copenhagen, Prague and Berlin. The next year she made another tour, this time with both Bohm and Nicholas Legat and in 1909 appeared briefly with Diaghilev's Ballets Russes during its first season in Paris.

Her relationship with the Imperial Theatre remained on a sound and amicable basis the while, for always she returned from her wanderings with an enhanced prestige for the Russian ballet as well as for herself. Even so, as far back as 1905 she gave some warning of her nature and temperament when she became a leader in a strike of young dancers at the Maryinsky. A group of dancers sought a larger degree of self-government, an aim for which the young Pavlova held boundless sympathy. In certain quarters her part in this puny and utterly ineffective fracas has been played down, her participation being excused as an act of loyalty to her colleagues and against her better nature. The facts themselves, at any rate outside Russia, are now obscure, if indeed they were ever anything but obscure, but I believe that she was an instigator and prime mover in the strike, for throughout her life she sought complete artistic independence. Although one can find countless examples of sympathy and loyalty for fellow artists in every phase of her career, never at any time did she make a single concession in her art or profession. This affair must to a twenty-five-year-old dancer, but recently become a ballerina, have been a serious matter indeed, and no amount of loyalty to her fellow artists would have induced her to fight any sort of battle against the authorities unless in the cause of artistic integrity.

The affair itself was of trifling importance. My sole reason for discussing it is to draw attention to the efforts, efforts which persisted all through her life and after, of some of her misguided admirers and adulators to overpaint with rosy, apologetic colours any acts or characteristics which might bring her down from the celestial heights in which she was at times almost lost to the common view. In making her out a goddess these people did less than justice to a great artist who was equally a woman.

It seems nevertheless that even those who were not prone to look at dancers through the mists of unreality were on occasion reduced when speaking or writing of Pavlova to employ terms of unwonted extravagance. In his *Reminiscences of the Russian Ballet*, for instance, Alexandre Bénois refers to the dance duet of Nijinsky and Pavlova in *Les Sylphides*:

> . . . with its high, noiseless, soaring flights, full of a tender delicate grace, conveyed the impression of a strange romance "beyond the grave," the hopeless love of bodiless spirits, who knew neither fiery embraces nor the sweetness of kisses, for whom all passion is replaced by sad caresses and soft, tremulous flitting . . .

But that eulogy becomes almost cold scientific analysis

beside the maudlin slush that filled the ladies' magazines and other periodicals as Pavlova began to capture the world's imagination. In studying the great masses of press cuttings which so many of her admirers devotedly collected and preserved in beautifully bound volumes I have been amazed at the extent of this "imaginative" writing. Before abandoning the count I discovered sixteen different writers who referred to her in that most hackneyed of all Terpsichorean clichés: "She danced with every fibre of her being." One poetically inspired critic described her as a "divine emanation," another as "a princess of melodious vision" and yet another as "music made visible." The phrase "poetry of motion" naturally coloured many a minor epic on this phenomenal creature and there was an output of the most unbelievable poetry that can ever have been inspired by one woman—even a dancer.

> Anna Pavlova, thy name is a spell that to our ears recalls
> Sweet soft sounds of the doves cooing by old shadowy walls.

What an anthology it would make. I wonder sometimes that the poor woman was not completely submerged in all this nonsense. It says much for the quality of her greatness that she could rise above this never-ending stream of cant, humbug, and "inspired" rubbish. Had her integrity been in the slightest degree assailable her work must have suffered under the sheer weight of its impact.

During one of her tours in Europe she was seen by the director of the New York Metropolitan Opera, who immediately signed her for a month's season. She appeared in New York for the first time in 1910. Here the touch of her foot and the flutter of her arms turned everything into dollars. Yet in spite of the vast sums she earned in the U.S.A.

no taint of vulgarity marked any of her activities, either on stage or off stage. It was the custom then almost as much as it is today for famous personalities to lend the lustre of their names, for enviable sums of course, towards the promotion of the sale of breakfast foods and patent medicines; but although she was constantly besieged by tempting offers, Pavlova never permitted her name to be used in this way. Her agents and impresarios obtained publicity for her by far more judicious and dignified but nevertheless extremely successful methods. Sol Hurok, too, the famous American impresario who promoted her tours in the U.S.A., although he kept her name continuously in bright lights, illumined only her fame, and never employed sensational stunts.

Throughout her life Pavlova shrank from any kind of scandal. From what little evidence remains available today I do not doubt that this warm and passionate creature had her affairs of the heart, but far from flaunting them she regarded them as essentially of a private and even sacred nature. Any tinge of scandal would have cheapened her to herself and throughout her life her own opinion of herself remained far more important to her than the opinion of others.

> An artist should never marry, yet I had to marry him (Victor Dandré), to please my English friends,

she said, but had she really meant this she would surely have allowed the marriage to have been publicly announced at the time, not some years after it had taken place. It appears that even members of her company travelling the world with her were surprised when they knew.

She very rarely gave way to emotionally charged statements, although of course every one of the women's periodicals of the time were constantly seeking crumbs from her lips. On one occasion, however, she did permit herself to say

> The right husband—he is the music for the wife's dance of life.

Her London début came a few months after that in New York, in April 1910, when she was booked by Sir Alfred Butt to appear at the Palace Theatre.

> I brought her to the Palace at £160 a week,

said Sir Alfred,

> she achieved, in a single night, the greatest success of any artist in my memory. She was a sensation overnight and soon I was paying her £1,200 a week.

During that first season Anna Pavlova and Michel Mordkin became the talk of the town. Not only the gossip columns but also the news pages of the national press were enlivened day after day by comments on the famous pair. Here is a typical extract from the *Pall Mall Gazette* of June 23rd, 1910:

> "Have you seen Pavlova?"
>
> The words have become almost a catch phrase. At the dinner tables or in the clubs, wherever two people meet together, the talk turns on Anna Pavlova and Michael Mordkin, the dancers from Russia, whose art is of a kind which has never before been seen in London.
>
> They have become a cult. People go to see them again and again. Their dancing is so wonderful that it is not enough to see them once. Just as you could look for ever on a beautiful picture, or never tire of the Venus de Milo, or read and reread some masterpiece of literature, so the desire to see Anna Pavlova and Michael Mordkin is luring people of all classes to the Palace Theatre.
>
> There have been world-famous entertainers at this house before; there have been sensations of a season, but never until to-day has there been a sensation of a century. That is why, every night at about ten o'clock,

> motor-cars and carriages arrive at the Palace and set down stately women in beautiful dresses who are content to stand at the back of the stalls, for there are no seats left, rather than forego the wonder and the fascination of the dancers.

After the success of her first American tour, when Pavlova danced with Mordkin, and his wife Potzitskia danced the character numbers in their repertoire, Pavlova decided to form her own company.

Before this second tour of the United States and Canada she appeared at the Metropolitan Opera in New York and such was the sensation she caused, that the most envied people in the country were those fortunate enough to have been able to buy a ticket for one of her performances.

During this season, with Mordkin as her partner, she was supported by some members of the Imperial Russian Ballet. The dancers who formed the ensemble were chosen by Pavlova by the holding of auditions. It was arranged that Albertieri, then ballet master of the Metropolitan Opera should rehearse this new *corps de ballet* but he in his turn asked an artist then appearing at the Hippodrome, New York, to take his place on many occasions. On seeing his deputy, Anna Pruzina, at work Pavlova, quick to recognise talent, realised at once that this artist would be an asset to the company she was about to form and without loss of time she invited her to join this company. Having accepted with delight, she and Pavlova became close friends and remained attached to one another till the end of Pavlova's life.

This original company numbered only ten. They were: Hilda Buick, an English girl who spoke many languages fluently, including Russian, which enabled her to act as interpreter for the others when necessary and Potzkovetska,

Kuhn, Schmoltz and Pruzina. Their partners were Morosov, Barbo, West, Cavitski and Mihaelovitch.

In 1911 Pavlova and Mordkin again appeared at the Palace Theatre. They also accomplished a long tour of America and in October Pavlova appeared briefly with the Diaghilev company in London, when she made her début at the Royal Opera House. All this time she was appearing in Russia at the Maryinsky Theatre for two months each year, for she did not resign her Russian commitments until 1913.

Indeed, she kept a large flat in Petrograd in which she maintained a practice room about forty-five feet long by thirty feet wide.

With the Diaghilev Ballet in London Pavlova danced in several works including *Giselle* and *Cléopatre*, being partnered by Nijinsky, but this was her last appearance with the famous Ballets Russes. In spite of her great artistic success with Diaghilev, it was inevitable that she would not remain long with that great company. Unlike her distinguished colleague Karsavina, her personality and temperament demanded that she remain always the dominating figure. With Diaghilev of course this could not be. He employed his dancers as an integral part of the ballet as a whole. Sometimes, because of the vital part played by music and the decorative arts in his great ballet renaissance, the dancers became indeed of only secondary importance. Pavlova was even more dedicated to the ballet than Diaghilev, but she saw its future from an entirely different point of view. To her ballet, ballet with the accent on dance, was a religion, to be taken to the peoples of the world through the instrument of her own personality, not through an organisation in which she would be but one factor, however important. Again unlike Karsavina, Pavlova did not come for any length of time directly under the cultural influence of

Diaghilev. As a result of that influence Karsavina was able to see ballet as more than dancing, whereas to Pavlova the sole means of communication lay in dance as distinct from ballet.

But there was even more to it than that. Neither Diaghilev nor Pavlova was noted for an ability to see the other's point of view. As one of her dancers said:

> . . . to work with her was like being a disciple of a Messiah. She regarded herself as infallible.

At the end of the 1911 season in London Mordkin left Pavlova and his place as her partner was taken by Novikov. Not only were there the performances at the Palace Theatre but many noble families vied with one another for Pavlova to appear as guest artist at their balls and receptions. Shortly after she acquired Ivy House the great ballerina gave a house-warming party at which she, partnered by Novikov and with the support of her small company, entertained her guests on the lawns.

During one season in London Pavlova thought she would like to find some talented children to dance in *Snowflakes*. After holding auditions she was surprised to see one of the rejected children come towards her and with tears in her eyes ask why she also could not be a "Snowflake." The little girl was small and fair and her charm instantly appealed to the ballerina.

"But, what can you do?" she asked the child.

"Look, I will show you," came the prompt reply. "I can run on the tips of my toes too." And without loss of time she was crossing the stage *sur les pointes* with grace and ease. Pavlova was enchanted and succumbed to the child's naïve charm. Her name was June, later to become a star of musical comedy.

For a large part of her career she seemed quite incapable of understanding that others might have a different opinion from her own. To her, once convinced of the rightness of a course of action, there was no other conceivable outlook. As a rule it was useless to remonstrate with her. Those who did found themselves overwhelmed by vehement contradiction and even on occasions abuse.

In time she would occasionally change her point of view. Perhaps this new outlook would be brought about by those who had differed from her in the first place, but rarely would she admit that she had been thus influenced. Indeed, she was probably quite unaware of having changed her opinion, much less of having given way to the impact of other opinions. But nobody who worked with her minded that, for almost without exception they worshipped her and the mere fact that she had for once adopted their point of view was in itself more than adequate repayment.

At the declaration of the first world war in 1914 Pavlova was in Berlin, but she managed to reach England *via* Belgium, where she assembled a company and went to the U.S.A. There she spent the next five years touring both North and South America with a company of about twenty-two dancers.

During the next eleven years she and her company travelled nearly all over the world, visiting every country in Europe. They went repeatedly to the U.S.A., Canada, Argentina, Brazil, Chile, Costa Rica, Cuba, Ecuador, Panama, Peru, Puerto Rico, Uruguay, Venezuela, Mexico, China, Japan, the Philippines, Malay States, Burma, India, Egypt, South Africa, Australia, New Zealand, and Java.

It is estimated that throughout her career she travelled about 500,000 miles, giving thousands of performances before millions of people. To most of them she represented an introduction to ballet, for she was the only dancer they had ever seen. Undeniably Pavlova more than anyone else interested the world in ballet and inspired young people themselves to dance. The result of this inspiration is to be seen today. The work entailed in these long tours is hard to imagine. Here I can convey it only by means of bald figures. During one tour of the U.S.A. in 1925 her company appeared in 77 towns during 26 weeks, giving 238 performances. She herself did not miss one of them. In every country she visited she was received and entertained by the leaders, whether kings, presidents, viceroys, or mayors. In Madrid the King of Spain sent a nightly bouquet to her dressing-room. In Canada she received a golden key and the freedom of the City of Quebec; in Venezuela a magnificent jewel case from the President. In Huddersfield the town council considered the occasion of her visit with careful deliberation and had a performance stopped so that the mayor, clad in all the authority of his chain of office, could make her an address of welcome—and present her with a bottle of vodka.

Popular magazines were no more averse then than now to publishing figures that were sensational if not necessarily accurate. It was claimed of Pavlova, during one particularly busy period in her life, that she earned £600 a night and used up 2,000 shoes a year. Probably, like so many of these stories, there is a basis of truth in it; one contract at least did bring her a financial reward somewhere in this fabulous region; and it is possible that her orders to Nicolini, the Italian shoemaker to whom she always gave her patronage, would have averaged at the rate of 2,000 pairs a year during one exceptional season. But not even Pavlova would have used up over five pairs a night for very long.

When starting a long tour it was her custom to take along an enormous number of shoes and when a couple of days from port to fit them all on. In a short while dozens and dozens lay on the floor, discarded as unsuitable after a few seconds' trial. These she distributed among the company.

Dancers do not normally expect to indulge in adventurous escapades, yet it is hardly surprising that in some of the remote places visited by Pavlova and her devoted group they found adventure, amusement and sometimes even danger. In Guayaquil, Ecuador, for instance, there was an epidemic of yellow fever when the company were due to appear there. Pavlova was warned not to make the visit, but nothing could deter her. Members of the company to this day recount the extraordinary precautions in regard to washing and drinking that had to be taken, but nobody contracted the dread fever. In Mexico there was a law regarding open air performances to the effect that if it rained during the first forty minutes the performance must continue regardless of the elements, otherwise it was obligatory to return the money to the audience. Pavlova was dancing *Le Cygne* on one occasion when there came a deluge. The company rushed for shelter but Madame, fully conversant with the law, completed her dance.

Frequently during her tours she visited out of the way areas which nobody ever appeared to have heard of before. Disdaining the beaten track she was quite happy to carry out her pioneering work anywhere it was possible for her to dance before an audience that had expressed a desire to see her. But it was not necessarily romantic travel she sought. Here, for example, is a typical itinerary of one of her tours through England, from October 3rd to December 10th, 1927:

First Week: Margate, Folkestone, Hastings, Brighton, Eastbourne, Shanklin (I. of W.), Bournemouth.

Second Week: Leicester, Nottingham, Derby, Sheffield, Leeds, Halifax.

Third Week: Huddersfield, Bradford, Blackburn, Llandudno, Hanley.

Fourth Week: Manchester, Warrington, Liverpool, Preston.

Fifth Week: Birmingham.

Sixth Week: Glasgow, Dundee, Aberdeen, Perth, Edinburgh.

Seventh Week: Newcastle, Middlesbrough, West Hartlepool, Darlington, York, Hull.

Eighth Week: Newark, Oxford, Portsmouth, Bournemouth.

Ninth Week: Bristol, Cardiff, Swansea, Plymouth, Torquay, Exeter.

Tenth Week: Cheltenham, Kidderminster, Worcester, Rugby.

Having studied a number of her itineraries as well as the programmes, I have come to the conclusion that she was the most hardworking dancer of all time. From Bundaberg to Kidderminster, Tennessee to Llandudno, the Royal Opera House, Covent Garden, to a bullring in Mexico, from dingy assembly halls to Europe's grandest theatres, her life consisted of work. Her "girls" still speak with bated breath of her vitality; lost in wonder they vie with each other in recounting tales of Madame practising in darkened theatres when everyone else was exhausted. According to present-day standards these girls themselves worked fabulously hard, but never half as hard or for such long periods as Pavlova.

> It is useless to dabble in beauty. One must be utterly devoted to beauty, with every nerve of the body.

Pavlova certainly lived up to this, her own dictum.

From what little she said on the subject, however, throughout her wanderings she often wanted to return to her native Russia. She gave her widowed mother there a regular and liberal allowance, except when through no fault of her own the Soviet Government returned it with a statement to the effect that they would not permit "bourgeois" charity in their great country. But if Russia always remained the home of her dreams, Ivy House, London, once the home of James Turner, the famous English landscape painter, became her real home. A solid, typically English structure at Hampstead Heath, Ivy House allowed Pavlova all the spaciousness she needed, for as well as possessing large and lofty rooms, it was set in about six acres of ground. The lawn sloped gently down through formal gardens to an artificial lake where Pavlova kept her famous swans. Gradually, amid loved belongings and creature comfort, the great dancer developed the stability and sense of security which must often have been lacking in one who spent so much time living in boats, trains, and hotel bedrooms. During her brief rests here, before embarking on yet another stupendous journey, she frequently entertained her friends and sometimes gave quite large garden parties. On intimate occasions she was the perfect hostess, treating everyone as a guest of honour, although rarely as a conventional English hostess would be expected to behave. Sometimes at lunch she would have the adjoining doors to her studio thrown open so that she could watch the progress of a class or rehearsal. At Ivy House, too, for a while she gave classes, but had to abandon them because of her lengthy absences. Just before her death she had ordered 8,000 tulips to be planted in her gardens, and it is perhaps in these gardens that some of her friends remember her in her most relaxed moments. Here she would plan wonderful if impossible holidays, in the course of a few moments producing the maddest schemes to be in several places at the same time.

In spite of her carefully cultivated English environment, and a gaiety which also became largely English in its characteristics, she never ceased to be and to think as a Russian. Her menu consisted of such items as black bread, buckwheat, rissoles in sour cream, and sturgeon. She also had a Russian chef, Vladimir, who made spasmodic appearances during important meals, ostensibly to enquire "if Madame wanted anything else," but really to solicit approbation. She was very interested in food, in common with all dancers, but although partial to ample variety, mostly contented herself with modest quantities. Throughout these meals which she enjoyed with her friends her high, chirrupy, but rhythmic and animated voice was constantly to be heard.

Even when enjoying a short respite between arduous tours, however, she spent much of her time at work. Daily practice was, of course, never neglected. Then there were rehearsals, interviews and auditions, photographs, fittings and all the normal work of supervising such an undertaking. Dandré, as he clearly demonstrated in his biography, loved Pavlova as his wife and worshipped her as an artist. Like everyone else associated with her he also worked tremendously hard in her interests, but always final decisions had to be left to Madame. No matter how strenuous the tour, how irksome the travelling or how inconvenient the environment, she insisted upon thorough and regular practice for every member of the company, but always herself doing more practice than the others.

> To strive tirelessly and at all times to reach one's goal —therein lies the secret of success. But what, actually, is success? I do not find it in the applause of audiences, but in the satisfaction at having realised an ideal. When, as a child wandering under those century-old pines, I foolishly thought that fame constituted happiness, I was in error. Fame is like a butterfly—its appearance charms you for a moment and then both the butterfly and the charm vanish.

Members of her company can recall frequent occasions when she displayed displeasure, and even anger, with audiences who applauded her indiscriminately when in her own opinion she had fallen beneath her own standards. But then she was continually dancing for uncritical and monotonously enthusiastic audiences; had she not perpetually striven for her own ideal of perfection, but sought only the adulation of indiscriminate masses, her standards must inevitably have fallen. In common with so many great artists she found praise a corrupting influence, but in spite of her efforts she still could not do without it. During one performance in Germany, with the Emperor present, which meant that the audience could not applaud, Pavlova, being unaware of this custom, was bitterly chagrined. Judging from accounts and opinions of such incidents, however, she rarely valued her tremendous popularity, apart from the fact that it brought people flocking to see her dance.

Her work itself of course was completely Russian, although she defined the Russian school as a mixture of the Italian school with all that is good of the French school, combined with the peculiar temperament of the Russians themselves.

After those early efforts to match the technical virtuosity of Legnani and others she followed the advice of Guerdt and made technique her servant rather than her mistress. But those who urge today that her technique was weak are either speaking in complete ignorance of the facts or else attempting pusillanimously to rob a dancer they have never seen of some of her greatness. In fact she had a very strong *pointe* which, together with that wonderful arched instep, was often photographed. Had she been born fifty years earlier she might have inspired Théophile Gautier when he said:

> If the foot is small, well arched, and falls on its pointe, like an arrow, if the leg, dazzling and pure, moves voluptuously amid the haze of muslin, we are not at all exercised about the rest.

Together with this strong and dazzling *pointe*, Pavlova possessed remarkable poise and balance and could hold almost indefinitely those beautiful arabesques. Unlike certain dancers of the present day, however, she never sought to dazzle with mere displays of technique, but always conditioned her dancing to what she considered to be the emotional demands of the moment.

At the outset of her career this sense of balance and poise made her brilliant in adage. Her *pas de bourées sur les pointes* across the stage, too, were so rapid and so smooth that she did appear to be skimming through the air.

She does not dance, she flies, said Diaghilev.

To attempt to sum up, much less to express the quality of her dancing, is to attempt the impossible. Perhaps the most apt words on the subject were those uttered by Karsavina, shortly after Pavlova's death.

> . . . where so many dancers are content to please by brilliance and gaiety, Pavlova conquered by her inimitable grace, her delicacy, some indefinable faery quality, something spiritual and exclusive to herself.
>
> To my mind she was the very spirit of romantic beauty in dancing, and those ethereal qualities of hers were never more finely exemplified than in *Les Sylphides* and *Le Cygne* . . . many people have spoken of the particular grace of her arm movements. That was part of her essential personal gift, and it was probably unique. She employed it, as she employed all her other movements, as the servant of that inward informing spirit which was the mainspring of her wonderful interpretations.

Throughout her career Pavlova studied as often as possible

In *Coppélia* at the outset of her stage career at the Maryinsky

In *La Bayadère* at St. Petersburg. This picture was used in connection with advance publicity matter for the first season of Diaghilev's Ballets Russes in Paris. At this time Pavlova was a *prima ballerina* at the Maryinsky with Cecchetti. During her holidays she quite often went to Milan to work under his eagle eye and Cecchetti always saw every one of her performances when she was dancing in Milan. Once, after watching her give an even more than usually inspired performance, he said:

> I can teach everything connected with dancing, but Pavlova has that which can be taught only by God.

She was strongly opposed to the use of a mirror in class, urging that by looking at it to check a pose one automatically falsified the line of that pose. She had many interesting and some profound theories on training and it is to be regretted that she never found time to codify them. It is even more to be regretted that so few dancers and teachers today possess her mental outlook towards classical dance.

> The study of classical dancing has intellectual as well as physical advantages. Educate children by having them interpret poems and stories and historical pageants, and you will give them an intellectual uplift and understanding which they can get in no other way.

At the beginning of her career as a ballerina she became an enthusiastic follower of Fokine's principles and, surprisingly enough, the supporters of the academic ballet of that time regarded her as a revolutionary. With Fokine she believed in the complete integration of dance and mime and was strongly opposed to the exploitation of dance for the sake of dancing without any emotional motivation. In this, then, she supported Fokine in his revulsion against the classical formula of the late nineteenth century; and she more than any other was responsible for presenting these particular Fokine principles to early twentieth-century audiences. But then, during the height of her career Diaghilev and his collaborators had taken those principles and stretched them into something quite new. In this of course Pavlova had no part and had no sympathy with the more extreme of the Diaghilevian innovations. By the supporters of Diaghilev she was now regarded as a reactionary. It was this unbridgable gap between her outlook and that of Diaghilev rather than any personal disagreements, which prompted her to ask people (see Arnold Haskell's letter on another page) that forthright question:

"Are you on my side or Diaghilev's?"

Although she had appeared only briefly with Diaghilev she had undeniably added to the brilliance and excitement of his revelation to the western world, but following that the two went their own divergent ways, each as a remarkable and persistent pioneer.

Many of the dances she performed were variations from the old classic ballets, but given with her own special interpretation. Mostly the décor and costumes she employed were undistinguished, as was common in pre-Diaghilev theatrical presentation and it was always her own dancing which was the constant focal point. She employed practically all English girls in her company. Her detractors have attempted to find capital in this, for they claim that English girls at that time were inferior dancers and that this gave Pavlova an opportunity to shine more than ever against a background of mediocrity. In fact this is quite untrue, for many of those girls were excellent dancers and made a reputation for themselves in their own right. A number of them are today distinguished teachers with very high reputations, some of them in America and some in England. The truth of the matter is that Pavlova's temperament was enough for one company. English girls, with their equable characters, became clay of an ideal consistency in her hands, moulding themselves to her will without that kind of resistance which so often begets exhausting and searing conflict between artists from more passionate lands.

There was a further reason. The dancers from the Imperial Russian Ballet with whom she started her company were permitted to be absent from Russia only for short periods. This meant that the personnel of the company was constantly changing. After her second season at the Palace Theatre in 1913, therefore, she decided to recruit her *corps de ballet* solely from English dancers.

When in England she spent countless hours visiting dance schools, sometimes to hold formal auditions, but at others just to watch the classes and pick out potential members for her company. Never was she known to refuse to look at any candidate; quite frequently, upon finding a girl candidate unsuitable, she would offer valuable advice. To all the members of her company she was a kindly, aristocratic martinet, although that description may suggest a contradiction in terms. With no children of her own, she became for long periods virtually the mother of her young English girls, practically all of whom came from good middle class English families and who had mostly never been out of England before they joined her company. At any rate, if they had, it must have been merely for genteel educational purposes to the Continent. Several of those girls, some of them now married women with families, have told me of the great struggle they had with their parents to win permission to go with Pavlova; of their sleepless nights waiting for the great parental decision; and of maternal tears and admonitions before embarkation. It speaks much for Pavlova that ultimately none of those parents regretted their decision, indeed some of them later expressed their gratitude to Madame for showing their children the world and awakening them to some of its treasures.

With her girls, as indeed with everyone else, Pavlova could be one moment the most generous and the next moment the most mean of women. Christmases and sometimes birthdays were marked by beautiful, appropriate and expensive presents, chosen by herself and given over some little celebration. On the other hand a few minutes after an outburst of remarkable generosity she would haggle doggedly over sixpence. Dandré as her business manager did his best to carry out her precepts in regard to finance, sometimes with the most delightful results. On one occasion, a girl injured her foot and was informed by the doctor that she would be unable to dance for several weeks. Dandré, on behalf of Madame and speaking in his most businesslike manner, explained to her that according to the terms of her contract she could either receive her full salary week by week and pay her own doctor's bills or alternatively the company would pay the bills and pay her the balance. As the girl had never even been given a contract—in fact I believe that no contracts were ever possessed by any member of the company—she was naturally a little puzzled, but decided to play safe and let the company pay the bills. On the following pay day, when Dandré gave her her usual remuneration with no deductions, she was honest enough to remind him of the arrangement. Dandré merely shrugged his shoulders. "Oh, don't worry about that," he said, "that has all been arranged."

For another month the girl continued to receive her full salary, although she remained inactive throughout this period.

Pavlova was perhaps best remembered for her impersonations of living but non-human creatures: a bird, an insect, a swan, a butterfly, a dragonfly. Mostly her ballets were solo dances or *pas de deux* with a *corps de ballet* background. Because of this it is often overlooked that she did in fact include some longer and quite lavish productions in her repertory; and that her expressions of various kinds and degrees of human emotion provided audiences the world over with an unforgettable experience. It is undeniable that these works usually lacked unity and cohesion and that audiences waited with more or less patience for Pavlova to reappear, but have we advanced so much further today? Do not a very large proportion of the audience at Covent Garden sit with resignation through the first act of *Swan Lake* and *The Sleeping Beauty*, waiting for Fonteyn at last to make her appearance? Pavlova was dancing throughout the world before audiences which were less conditioned to ballet than those of today.

Even so, she did sometimes present ballets which were the occasion for nine- or ten-inch reviews in *The Times* and other quality periodicals. Here is an extract from a review which appeared in *The Times* after her presentation of *Giselle* at Covent Garden in 1924.

> Mme. Pavlova began at Covent Garden last night her four weeks' season of ballet (a season in which she promises some variation in each night's programme) with a classic of the choreographic stage, Adam's *Giselle*. In the forties *Giselle* gave to Carlotta Grisi one of her richest opportunities, and now its revival is welcome because it gives us more of Mme. Pavlova in the hour and a half that it takes to play than does any other work of its length.
>
> We may smile a little at the pale romanticism of Théophile Gautier's scenario, and scarcely trouble to let Adam's tunes take sufficient hold of us to make us whistle a bit of one of them as we go home. But the one gives us situations in which Mme. Pavlova can be lavish with her charms, the other provides measures to which her steps may really move. Perhaps the chief delight of her

> performance to the musical mind was the ease with which all her wealth of technical resource as a dancer kept its relation to the simple, almost childish, rhythm of the music.
>
> The first scene of *Giselle* allows Mme. Pavlova to exercise all her art in the expression of artlessness; the village maiden, happy with her love, sporting with her friends, admiring the princess. Next come disillusionment, tragedy, madness, and death. By the end of this first act the ballet would seem to have exhausted the gamut of emotions. We begin to think we have seen Mme. Pavlova in every phase, and the fall of the curtain leaves us wondering how all that elaboration of rhythmic movement could adapt itself so perfectly to such diverse emotional ends.
>
> But the resources are not exhausted. Romanticism has its advantages, for it can resuscitate Mme. Pavlova and bring her back as a peculiarly agile ghost and so provide a second act of still more coruscating pirouettings. To all this everyone else made a mere shadowy background; M. Laurent Novikov, the devout lover, who was always ready to balance her on one toe or lift her over his head, whether as simple village maiden or as disembodied spirit; M. Clustime, whose villainy produced her mad scene; the *corps de ballet* of vintage girls in Act I and of ill-omened spirits in Act II. All were quite efficient, and the spirit maidens had the additional usefulness of showing how big a gap there is between their conventional grace and her unique perfection.

The sets for these long ballets aimed largely at a quasi-naturalism rather than artistic invention. In *Don Quixote*, for example, Rosinante was played by a real horse. Although petted, pampered and fattened by every member of the company, who constantly fed it with titbits, this creature was so ingeniously made-up that on-stage he did actually bear some resemblance to the emaciated creature of Cervantes' imagination. So convincing was his appearance that certain members of the audience complained to the R.S.P.C.A. who sent an inspector to investigate.

But for the most part Pavlova won the adulation of the world through her romantic and emotional interpretations of short and well-known pieces. It seemed that the more familiar audiences became with such works as *Le Cygne* and *Papillon* the more exciting they found them, for Pavlova's interpretations themselves never staled into a familiar and outworn formula. Frequently she found a new subtlety of interpretation in each of her dances.

According to many of her colleagues Pavlova constantly desired to create certain modern works, but felt that her public would not favour such works. From time to time she discussed the possibilities of such projects with whatever partner she happened to have at the time. Stowitts, for instance, wrote the following:

> On our way to South America we walked the decks together for hours discussing ballets we wanted to do. Sometimes she would cry because she was not permitted to experiment, to be modern, to do the new things that she wanted to do . . . she wanted to do modern ballets that we outlined together. She realised that most people thought she could only do the conventional—the traditional dances—and that hurt her. . . . Pavlova was just as sorry as the rest of us that the prestige of her company was lowered by such inferior choreographers . . . who, although they trained the artists in a good conventional school, were also permitted to arrange the dances; whereas neither of them has any great ability, and merely imitated pseudo fashion ballets which they had seen elsewhere. But the fault was in no way Pavlova's, because in every instance she added to . . . choreography some extraordinary touch of her own which transformed it completely . . .

But when one is a pioneer of the nature of Pavlova,

bringing the beauty of the dance to large masses, as distinct from Diaghilev who sought to excite the cultured few, one's own more advanced aims and ambitions have to be ruthlessly suppressed. Diaghilev once said:

> The longer a work of genius remains hidden from the enthusiasms of the multitude the more complete and more intact will it remain for the lovers of true art.

whereas Pavlova believed that it was her great mission to take the art of which she was the chosen vessel far and wide. She said:

> I want to dance for everybody in the world.

Because she took ballet not only to places where it was hitherto unknown, but also because large sections of her audiences regarded it merely as another act in a variety bill, she had to be careful not to lay herself open to the laughter and ridicule of the philistines. Nevertheless, once or twice she could not resist a temptation to produce a modern work without concession to popular taste. In 1912 she produced on original lines *The Three Palms*, with music by Spendiarov. This contained a number of departures from her accepted style, but although her own performance was enthusiastically applauded, the work itself failed to please either the critics or the public. *Ajanta Frescoes*, which she built on a foundation of Hindu mythology, after becoming deeply interested in Indian art, dancing and music, was also a work in advance of its times. Here much of the movement was composed of abstract and highly stylised gestures unacceptable to the great public who loved her and made her their slave. Yet another work which those who dimly remember it today speak of in terms of high artistic accomplishment was Novikov's *Russian Folklore*, set to Tcherepnine music. This too was not very enthusiastically received. Another work of an advanced

Pavlova with her group of pupils in a picture taken a little while before the First World War

The oil and pastel portrait by Savely Sorin, the Russian artist. This portrait was much admired during the Diaghilev Exhibition at Forbes House at the end of 1954

The Swan

With Varjinsky in *Gavotte Pavlova*

Rondino. The original costume, which was later replaced by the better known lilac one. This costume was however again favoured by Pavlova when she wore it for *Blue Mazurka* in 1928

nature, with a set that was transformed simply by a change of lighting, was *Dionysus*, by Tcherepnine.

The only complete ballet designed and arranged by Pavlova herself was *Autumn Leaves*. I never saw it but even if I had I doubt very much whether today I should be able to remember it well enough to make any worthwhile comment on the choreography. The difficulty of bringing back to mind such a transitory and elusive thing as choreography is amply testified by the difficulties experienced in their attempts to revive this ballet by a group of Pavlova's company who danced in it many times. I think their efforts have been to a certain extent fruitful, but when a group who have actually performed the ballet so many times themselves find difficulty in reconstructing it, how can a mere member of the audience, no matter how experienced, perceptive and long-memoried, hope to revive it accurately enough in his mind's eye to be able to say anything worthwhile about it?

Yet there are still people who believe they can make fair and accurate comparisons between a ballet of today and its prototype of twenty-five years ago, between the dancing of Pavlova and the dancing of Fonteyn!

Those who seek to smear the wonderful legend of Pavlova quote against her a lack of creative ability. What nonsense! How many compositions have Yehudi Menuhin and Margot Fonteyn to their credit? Are they any the less great as interpretative artists because of this absence of activity in the creative field?

Another factor often quoted to the detriment of Pavlova is the triviality of the themes on which so many of her short works were constructed. Again this is a criticism which can easily be refuted by reference to the programme notes of every company in existence today. Does anyone claim that the themes for such works as *Madame Chrysanthème*, *The Lady and the Fool*, *House of Birds*, *Beauty and the Beast*, are much more than trivial? And does it necessarily mean that because of the triviality of their themes these works are in themselves of no account? It has been said that the beauty of a work depends on its form, its greatness on its content. This definition can aptly be applied to many ballets and to Pavlova's short works in particular. She employed trivial themes for non-trivial work; she is remembered for the beauty of her dancing rather than the greatness of her work.

The most famous of all her dances for example, *Le Cygne*, was in essence nothing more than a pretty, sentimental trifle, accompanied by hackneyed, sugary music; yet Pavlova's alchemy transformed these ingredients into one of the outstanding glories in the whole history of ballet. All too often in recent years we have seen what can happen to this same dance when it is attempted by lesser artists.

Fokine was Pavlova's ideal choreographer, for he seemed to understand exactly the type and style of movement which the great dancer could infuse with life. According to her own words Pavlova very rarely modified any of the arrangements Fokine made for her, but this cannot be said of any other choreographers. In the first place she was not very quick at learning a new dance. Her method as a rule was to master it in separate sequences and then to piece them together. Even then she sometimes forgot certain movements, especially if they appeared to her to follow no logical or dynamic pattern. Then she would interpolate her own variations. Similarly, when she had thoroughly mastered a dance, from time to time she modified it to suit her mood of the moment.

In common with most great interpretative artists these moods of hers changed and varied with great rapidity. Although she made deliberate efforts to prevent them from conditioning her work, naturally at times they did affect both the impetus of her dance itself and her own emotional reactions. Although none of the almost unbelievable number of photographs and paintings of her is able to express the tremendous vitality and passion of her nature, they do I think clearly portray, when looked at in sufficient number, this variety of her moods. This variety indeed seems to amount occasionally almost to a change in the actual shape of her face, which of course can be no more than an illusion, but it is a most convincing illusion. I do not know of any other dancer whose expressions are subject to such profound transitions.

Mostly the quality of the hundreds of paintings of the great dancer is deplorable. She was of course painted by nearly all the fashionable artists of her day: Sir James Lavery, Sir William Orpen and others whose work was in equal demand. None of these paintings rises above a superficial likeness, usually in highly romanticised style and sickly colour. A few artists did seek to penetrate beneath the surface and facing page 40 is reproduced one of these portraits, by the Russian artist Sorin. This portrait in no way lends false glamour to her classical features but stresses their contours and moulding so that the portrait expresses the essence of her character. It is perhaps not surprising that Pavlova herself disliked it, for in common with lesser people she was not able to see herself as others saw her.

Portrait painters, with the exception of a few in the very top rank, invariably lend enchantment to the view. It would have been strange indeed had Pavlova not come to believe in time that she really did closely resemble all the "glamorised" portraits of her executed by knights of the realm rather than those painted by artists with more profound vision.

There was also a considerable amount of trivial sculpture of Pavlova in her well-known dances, much of it being presented at the annual exhibitions of the Royal Academy. In Russia however the Czar Nicholas II actually bestowed upon Pavlova the great honour of commissioning Seraphin Soudbinine to create a bust of her. Further, he sent Soudbinine to London solely for this purpose. Later, models were reproduced from the original at the Czar's own private factory. Czar Nicholas had a great admiration for Pavlova. When she was about to embark on her first trip to Europe he bade her God speed but added:

> I am only afraid lest foreign countries should entice you away from Russia for too long.

Pavlova herself, for relaxation, sculptured a considerable number of small figures—all of them understandably of dance poses. Many of her porcelain statuettes are to be seen today. Although they possess a certain delicate charm and some of them a most attractive line, they are by no means great works of art. Their creator knew this as well as anybody and she was most reluctant at all times to have them copied or exhibited. She said:

> I cannot sign them. They are not good enough.

Because of her great variety of moods and constantly changing character, even those who were closest to her felt quite frequently that they scarcely knew her. One moment she would be the simplest of all creatures, taking delight in childish pleasures. Once she remained delighted for days after receiving an extract of a child's essay. This child had been to see Pavlova while on holiday and on returning to school had chosen this great treat as the subject for an essay. She started off:

> Once I saw a fairy. Her name was Anna Pavlova.

At other times Pavlova was the haughty, imperious, *ballerina assoluta*. Then all those around her had to exert tact and diplomacy and remain constantly on the alert, or they would find themselves in trouble. Her scenes with Mordkin during her 1911 season in London were subjected to much comment in the press. Some writers stated that Mordkin had dropped her and she had slapped his face (others claimed his arm was the target). Today, although the roots of the trouble undoubtedly went deeper than that, who knows the real facts? Certainly there had been no little friction between Mordkin and Pavlova. She received the vast bulk of the publicity and adulation and he was for the most part regarded merely as her partner, although he did have an extremely large following of admirers. The matter was further complicated through the fact that Mordkin's wife had danced at the Palace in 1910 and was offered a contract by Sir Alfred Butt to appear in 1911 with the Pavlova group. This contract she turned down on the grounds that she could not appear in a lesser rank than Pavlova. But whatever the various aggravations, the fundamental cause was manifestly once again the inevitable clash between two highly individualistic natures. The climax—that is the climax enacted before the public—offered much excitement, even if this excitement had little connection with ballet. Here is an eye-witness account written by "Tristram" in *The Referee* on August 6th, 1911:

> Last night—at Mr. Mordkin's final appearance at the Palace—excitement ruled lively, and the atmosphere was "electric," so to speak. It was evident from the state of the house that something in the nature of a "scene" was expected. The dances were gone through as per schedule. Mlle. Pavlova and her troupe and Mordkin each received loud plaudits and batches of floral tributes after each dance. In Mordkin's case some of the tributes

were fruity rather than floral, and included grapes, apples, and even a banana! These Mordkin proceeded to sample with apparent gusto.

Anon the final dance, "The Bacchanale," was reached, the dancers dancing together this time and receiving thunders of applause. Then came call after call, but each time the two dancers kept well apart. Mordkin seemed to get well in front for a time in the apparent race for curtain-calls. Towards the end he seemed to win on the number of calls. This was resented by some of the audience. Finally, however, Mlle. Pavlova got in front of the curtain again, and went off triumphantly.

There have also been various interpretations of the reasons for Hilda Butsova's departure from the Pavlova company in 1926. Butsova had become a *première danseuse* with the Pavlova Ballet, having previously been with Diaghilev. It is clear however from Butsova's own brief reminiscences, published in a woman's periodical, that her life, unlike the lives of her colleagues in the company, was not dominated solely by an unbounded adulation of Pavlova. When making up her mind as to whether to accept an invitation to join this company or another she said:

> I reasoned that it might not be difficult later to obtain a ballet of my own.

But soon the young dancer found that Pavlova was becoming too great an influence in her life. She wrote:

> It is impossible to watch Chopiniana, with its waltzes, preludes and mazurkas, or Don Quixote or Autumn Leaves or Amarilla danced thousands of times and not unconsciously imbibe many graces and fine points that belong to Madame. And need many of these delicate edges certainly I did, but eventually comes the moment when the bird must try its own wings, and it is a wise bird that knows that moment. Perhaps I should never have known my moment, but Madame in her wisdom

and generosity and kindness recognised it and pointed it out to me, and herewith is printed the letter that she sent me upon the occasion of our parting last autumn . . .

And here is one of Pavlova's few letters, written to Butsova:

My dear Hilda:

The sad moment of our parting has arrived after so many years spent in happy collaboration. From the depths of my heart I wish you the most complete success in your new life and I want to express to you my deep gratitude for the unfailing loyal and staunch attitude you have always shown towards my enterprise and its interests.

Beginning with a small part in corps de ballet, you have gradually worked your way up, until you have filled the principal role in a series of ballets, given in all parts of the world, visited during our long tours, and invariably you have helped me and been a success in the parts you have taken.

I have found in you, not only an excellent dancer, eager and ready to take up any new dance or role entrusted to her, but I have valued greatly also your kind and good-natured disposition, which has prompted you to enter so wholeheartedly into my interests. Your sterling character and your sincerity have made friends of all around you, and I am sure that the whole company will say good-bye to you with genuine and deep regret.

I cannot say more than that I hope you will remain just the same as you are now and will enjoy the most complete happiness in your new life.

My warmest good wishes go with you.

Anna Pavlova

On several occasions Butsova had solo parts given to her by Pavlova only to have them taken away and given to a new member of the company. She was by no means the only one to suffer in this way, and realised, as indeed did several of the other girls, that if she lost a part there must be some very good reason. Sometimes it took such deprivation to make them realise that extreme familiarity with a role had caused them to become slipshod both in its execution and interpretation. Pavlova herself must have had to fight against this tendency more than any other dancer in the world, for she performed her roles thousands and thousands of times. From her own experience she realised that the dancer is less likely to be able to detect her own blemishes and failings in a role which she feels that she has completely mastered than in one with which she is not so familiar and the full interpretation of which still eludes her.

Throughout her maturity Pavlova seemed to enjoy extreme contrasts. Although it is all too easy, for the purpose of furthering an argument, to find such contrasts where none really exist, it is I think fairly clear that her warm and intimate friendship with Charlie Chaplin is an example of what I mean. Her art lay in transcending humanity, his in stressing its pathos. She loved to swim but hers was a kind of swimming which was a ludicrous contradiction of the grace of her movements on stage. In fact Dandré and others sought always to prevent her from taking to the water, for there seemed to be a certain element of danger in her efforts. Instead of entering the swimming bath by sliding down into the water she liked to dive, invariably landing in a terrifying manner with a dreadful splash. Once she actually knocked herself out in this way, but remained undeterred and had to be watched carefully when swimming facilities were too conveniently situated.

She loved to gamble, although gambling was opposed to her nature, and she played poker with childish excitement. She had absolutely no card sense, according to Fokine who played many times with her, but grew naïvely excited when she won a few shillings.

Always she displayed interest in the primitive rites and rituals of the countries she visited, and became well versed in the national dances of several countries. On the other hand she loathed anything that appeared to her of a polyglot nature and therefore she could not tolerate jazz. Perhaps one of the best examples of the lengths to which she would go in order to see things for herself, is her visit to the notorious Barbary Coast. She heard about this district when in San Francisco and was determined to see some of the new dances she had heard about, such as the Turkey Trot and Grizzly Bear. Seeking help from her friends, who in order to minimise the risk, themselves consulted the Chief of Police, she arranged a visit to the Olympia, the most infamous of the rendezvous on the Barbary Coast. Here foregathered the crews of freighters and sailing ships from all over the seven seas and the Orient. Masquerading under the guise of a dance hall, the Olympia had a gold-painted interior in which a circular floor was surrounded by a raised platform. On this platform were constructed booths for spectators; while on the floor tom-toms, cymbals, horns and banjos urged a mass of unsavoury types into their weird dances. Sailors, pickpockets, dope fiends, negroes, and Mexicans in all types of attire, danced with streetwalkers.

Pavlova was fascinated by the spectacle and actually went on to the floor with Mordkin.

During her life the cinema, although it had already captured the world's fancy, could hardly be claimed to have become a highly developed art. Technically too it had barely begun to grope its way towards its wonderful achievements of today. Nevertheless Pavlova was deeply interested in this medium, both as a means of recording the dance and for her own self-criticism. She had a projector installed at Ivy House and frequently subjected herself to the far from flattering scrutiny of the cinema lens. She used to look at these films with great attention and have them run through time after time. Apparently she was most severely critical of her own performances and was able to learn much by this means.

It is a pity that only such a tiny fraction of the films made of her are still in existence. Some of those that do remain are from time to time shown to small audiences, but they do her scant justice. There are however some moments when at least some of her greatness can be sensed. Even such a hater of ballet as the late James Agate was able to appreciate her quality in this way. Shortly after her death, on viewing a film of *The Immortal Swan*, he expressed his exasperation at the lack of dancing in it. He said:

> Much of the dancing part of the Pavlova film, when we come to it at last, is quite lovely. There is a slow motion sequence, too, which is particularly valuable in that it shows Pavlova to have been incapable of ungracefulness even in the hundredth part of a second. The harrowing pathetic flutter of her arms in the famous Swan Dance must be classed among things of ageless beauty; one would only desire that the study of this film would ensure its being a joy for ever.

These films of Pavlova prompted many lovers of ballet in 1931 to urge that for the benefit of posterity more and more films should be made of great dancers and great ballets. Arnold Haskell, for example, once wrote:

> It is to be hoped that really good cinematograph records are being kept of Pavlova, so that the future may have that fairly accurate means of forming opinions which we lack in the case of famous Opéra dancers.

In spite of the wonderful technique of the cinematic

camera today, films of Margot Fonteyn fail lamentably to convey her personality; and they fail even more when they seek to portray her particular kind of physical beauty. It is therefore hardly surprising that those of Pavlova are even less valuable as a record or even a reminder of the great dancer. Nevertheless the cinema camera, in all the technical brilliance it has achieved in the last twenty-five years, can capture the line and dynamic, and sometimes the whole feeling and atmosphere of a dance. I sincerely hope therefore that before she retires Fonteyn will undertake to film at least some of her outstanding dances, so that future lovers of ballet will at least have a more accurate conception of her greatness than we have of Taglioni, Elssler, Karsavina or Pavlova.

Anna Pavlova, as is so well remembered by all those who saw her, and by many who did not, died on January 23rd, 1931, at the Hague, almost at the opening of a fresh tour. Undoubtedly she had started again too soon after a short illness which, added to the great tax she had imposed upon her limited strength over a number of years, proved too much for her.

The newspapers devoted more space to reports of her death, and later to obituary notices, than to any dancer before or since. Hosts of her admirers mourned her death at such a seemingly early age. Some of them continue to speak with infinite sadness of her to this day. But in fact this was no sad occasion. The great dancer had in the last two years of her life spoken more than once of retirement; had even planned to make one final tour of America before doing so. But would such a dedicated spirit have reaped any pleasure or satisfaction, much less found fulfilment, if unable to dance? Towards the end, although none in the audience could detect it, she was becoming physically exhausted at the end of each performance, panting for breath and almost collapsing as the curtain came down. This exhaustion was intensified by a disability in her knee, from which she had suffered for some years; further, that slender, expressive figure had begun to put on weight and odd remarks let slip revealed that she realised the signs that pointed towards the end of her career. Retirement? No. For such as Pavlova, who live in almost unceasing tension and intensity, longevity is no blessing but a sore scourge from which she was fortunate indeed to escape.

André Levinson wrote shortly after her death:

> Twenty, thirty times I spoke of her when she was alive. And always at the moment when I thought I had captured the miracle of her art and the mystery of her personality, words failed me. Technique can be analysed with perfect calm, talent can be examined from every angle, but before the revelation of genius the manifestation of the divine in a human being, one is left in a state of bewildered delight.

Diaghilev is remembered for his clearly manifest reforms in ballet; for the new impetus he brought to a corrupt art form. Pavlova made no such reforms, but through her own special genius brought throughout the world a new love for the dance, and a new impetus to the dance itself. What a tragedy it would have been had she herself outlived the spirit that inspired her.

Chapter Two

IMPRESARIO'S VIEWPOINT

Sol Hurok

IT was The Swan who determined my career in dance and ballet management. Whatever my aspirations on arriving in America towards the music and the dance, I had determined, after exciting days of presenting Chaliapine, Schumann-Heink, Eugene Ysaye, Mischa Elman, Tetrazzini and others in the concert world, to do for the dance what I had succeeded in doing for music.

It was then that I met The Swan.

Pavlova is a symbol of ballet in America; and, indeed, throughout the world. I felt that in America there were people who, if they could but know the dance, would love it, and the only way for them to know it was, I felt, to expose them to it in its finest form, the ballet.

Before the arrival of Anna Pavlova in the United States there had, to be sure, been sporadic displays of dancing; all of it imported from Europe and for the most part in fits and starts. From the time of Fanny Elssler's triumphs in the early 1840's until the arrival of Pavlova in 1910 there was a long balletic drought, relieved only by occasional showers.

America had not been reluctant to receive Fanny Elssler.

Her passionately dramatic tour was a delirium of enthusiasm. She was the guest of the President at the White House and Congress suspended its sittings on the days she danced. She was pelted with flowers. Red carpets were unrolled and spread before her. But all this was in the nature of an isolated instance.

It is my belief that the first appearance of Pavlova at the Metropolitan Opera House, New York, on February 28th, 1910, is a date to remember, since it may be said to mark the beginning of the ballet era in our country.

That first visit was made possible by the generosity of the late Otto H. Kahn, to whom the art world of America owes an incalculable debt. Her success at the Met was more remarkable because as an Italian opera director, Gatti-Cazzaza was not sympathetic to the dance, and was, moreover, extremely dubious that Metropolitan audiences would accept ballet, other than as an inconsequential *divertissement* during the course of an opera.

Because of his anti-dance attitude, and in order to play safe, Gatti ordained that Pavlova's American début be scheduled to follow a performance of Massenet's opera *Werther*. The Massenet opera being a fairly long three-act work, its final curtain did not fall until past eleven o'clock. By the time the stage was ready for the first American appearance of Pavlova, it was close to eleven-thirty. The audience that had remained largely out of curiosity rather than from any sense of expectation left reluctantly at the end. The dancing they had seen was like nothing ever shown before in the reasonably long history of the Metropolitan. For her début Pavlova had chosen Delibes' *Coppélia*, giving her in the role of Swanilda a part in which she excelled. The triumph was almost entirely Pavlova's. The role of Frantz allowed her partner, Mordkin, little opportunity for technical display, the *corps de ballet* seems to have been undistinguished, and the Metropolitan conductor, Podesti, most certainly was not a conductor for ballet, whatever else he might have been.

Altogether in this first season there were four performances of *Coppélia*, and two of *Hungary*, a ballet composed by Alexandre Glazounov. Additional works during a short tour that followed, and which included Boston and Baltimore, were the *Bacchanale* from Glazounov's *The Seasons*, and *La Mort du Cygne* (The Dying Swan), the miniature solo ballet Fokine had devised for her in 1905, which was to become her symbol.

Such was the success that Pavlova returned for a full season in New York and a subsequent tour the following autumn, bringing Mordkin's adaptation of *Giselle*, and another Mordkin work, *Azayae*.

It was six years later that The Swan floated into my life. In 1916, Charles B. Dillingham, Broadway theatrical producer with a difference, was the director of the Hippodrome, that unforgettable Sixth Avenue institution. Dillingham was "different" for a number of reasons. He was a theatre man of vision; the Hippodrome, with its fantastic and colossal entertainments, if not his idea, was his triumph; he was perhaps the only Broadway manager who had been offered the post of business manager of the Metropolitan Opera Company, an offer he refused, but he did accept a commission to make a complete survey of the Metropolitan's business affairs.

For years I had stood in awe of him.

In 1916, Dillingham engaged Pavlova to appear at the Hippodrome with her partner, Alexandre Volinine. Neither the auspices, the billing, nor the setting could, by any stretch of the imagination, be termed ideal. Dillingham's Hippodrome bore the subtitle "The National Amusement Institution of America," an appellation as grandiose as the building itself. The evening's entertainment (plus daily matinées), of which The Swan's appearance was a part, was billed as "The Big show, the Mammoth Minstrels, and the Ice Ballet, The Merry Doll."

So Pavlova was dancing at the Hippodrome. Along with the trained elephants and the acrobats, the Chinese jugglers and the nymphs who vanished in the disappearing tank, Pavlova was dancing to the music of Tchaikovsky.

Where Pavlova was, there was I. I was standing, as always, at the back of the house, watching her exquisitely poignant figure far away on the huge stage, a miniature from where I stood, like a figure seen through the wrong end of the telescope. I might as well have been on Mars, for all the hope I had of ever spanning the infinity between us.

And at the very moment, when it seemed intolerable any longer to worship from afar, as the curtain fell slowly on the fragile statuette, a hand grasped my arm.

"I'm going back to her dressing-room—come along, Sol," Dillingham said.

I had lost my awe of Charles B. Dillingham by then—we were both managers, after all—but at that moment he was God, or at the very least, Saint Peter.

The words that I would say to Anna Pavlova when I met her were ready on my tongue. I had polished and rehearsed them during the thousand times I had met her face to face in imagination. I had practised my speech in Russian, and I had practised it in English, and I had never made up my mind in which language my flowery eloquence would be most effective.

She sat before her dressing-table, a plain little red robe thrown over her shoulders. Dillingham's voice presenting me came from a million miles away.

With Mordkin in *Russian Dance*

Some action shots of *The Dragonfly*

A Japanese Dance

/ith Mordkin in *Valse Caprice*

With Stowitts in

Syrian Dance

With Pianovsky in

Mexican Dance

English or Russian, Russian or English? Which should I speak? I was pilloried by the dilemma. I stood dumb, silent, stupid, blanketed by a fog in which Russian words and English words ran together and became Sanskrit and ancient Greek.

She was smiling. She put out her hand to me and, like an automaton, I bent over it. When I straightened she was speaking to Dillingham.

"Let your friend come too," she said. "It will be gay, three of us."

So I had met Pavlova, and been invited by her to supper, and I had not said a single word.

Later, when Pavlova had been stranded with her company in South America by the war she was glad to find a haven in the United States. But as soon as the armistice was signed she was ready to go. Almost the first boat to England took her home to Ivy House. I did not see her off.

In 1920 I presented Fokine and Fokina at the Hippodrome and at the Metropolitan Opera House. One night at the Hippodrome Fortune Gallo came up to me.

"Well, Hurok, I'm going to be a competitor of yours," he said. "I'm going to bring Pavlova back to America next season."

Pavlova's own lawyer Goldberger, Gallo told me, had gone to London to make the deal for him.

I was bitter. But I was determined not to be left entirely in the cold. I offered to take the New England tour, and Gallo accepted. Actually, he managed only a small part of the tour himself. He sold the Midwestern tour to managers in the Middle West.

I did not go down to meet her at the boat, but during her week at the Manhattan Opera House I went to see her three times. In Boston I began to talk about the following season.

I met her in Detroit, went to Indianapolis and Chicago with her. After Chicago I had a signed contract for the next year in my pocket, and I was a happy man.

In the years that followed there developed a long and unforgettable association. Her first tour under my management, and large parts of others, we made together; and not, I may say, entirely for business reasons. Thus did I learn to know the real Anna Pavlova.

For those of a generation who know Pavlova only as a legend, there is a large library of books about her as artist and dancer. As for myself, I can only echo the opinion of J. L. Vaudoyer, the eminent French critic, when he said: "Pavlova means to the dance, what a Racine is to poetry; a Poussin to painting; a Gluck to music."

Unlike certain ballerinas of today, Pavlova never indulged in exhibitions of virtuosity for the mere sake of eliciting gasps from an audience. Hers was an exhibition of the traditional school at its best, a school famed for its soundness. Her balance was something almost incredible, but never was it used for circus effects. There was in everything she did an exquisite fluency and incomparable grace.

Above and beyond all this, I like to remember the great humanity and simplicity of Pavlova the woman. I have seen all sides of her character. There are those who could testify to a very human side. A friend of mine on being taken backstage at the Manhattan Opera House in New York to meet Pavlova for the first time, was greeted by a fusillade of ballet slippers being hurled with unerring aim, not at him, but at the departing back of her husband, Victor Dandré, all to the accompaniment of pungent Russian imprecations. Under the strain of constant performance and rehearsal she was human enough to be ill tempered. It was quite possible for her to be completely unreasonable.

On the other hand, there are innumerable instances of her warmheartedness, her generosity, her tenderness. Passionately fond of children, and denied any of her own, the tenderness and concern she showed for all children was touching. This took on a very practical expression in that she established and maintained a private home in Paris for some thirty-odd refugee children. This she supported, not only with money, but with the closest personal supervision.

Worldly things, money, jewellery, meant little to her. She was a truly simple person. Much of her valuable jewellery was rarely, if ever, worn. Most of it remained in a safe-deposit vault in a Broadway bank in New York City, where it was found only after her death.

Money was anything but a motivating force in her life. I remember her once when she was playing an engagement in Chicago. For some reason business was bad, very bad, as, on more than one occasion, it was. The public at this time was firmly staying away from the theatre. I was in a depressed mood, not only because expenses were high and receipts low, but because of the effect that half-empty houses might have on Pavlova and her spirits.

While I tried to put on a smiling front that night at supper after the performance, Pavlova soon penetrated my poker-faced veneer. She leaned across the table, took my hand.

"What's wrong, Hurokchik?" she asked.

"Nothing," I shrugged, with as much gallantry as I could muster.

She continued to regard me seriously for a moment. Then:

"Nonsense." She repeated it with her usual finality of emphasis. "Nonsense. I know what's wrong. Business is bad, and I'm to blame for it. . . . Look here . . . I don't want a penny, not a kopeck. . . . If you can manage, pay the boys and girls; but as for me, nothing. Nothing, do you understand? I don't want it, and I shan't take it."

After 1926 Pavlova did not return to America. She made her English and Continental tours, travelled to South Africa, to Australia, with a small company. I saw her in Europe every year.

In the summer of 1930 she telephoned me in Paris. I was taking the *Leviathan* back to the States in a few days. Wouldn't I come to Southampton, where they were playing, and spend some time with her before I left? I could board my boat at Southampton as well as at Cherbourg, couldn't I?

No invitation could have been more welcome. We spent four days together, wandering about the town, going to performances, playing poker. It was like old times.

She was thinking of bringing her small ensemble to America the next season. I was opposed to this and I said so.

"Well, since I'm not going to be your manager this time, I'm going to have a good time with you," I said. "I'll come back-stage and be your cavalier."

"Yes," she said, and then she began to cry. "I'm coming to see you off at the boat," she declared suddenly.

Dandré protested. She was due to leave for another town on her provincial tour.

"I have to see that he has a nice stateroom," she insisted.

I tried to dissuade her. "It's so damp at the dock; you might catch a cold," I said.

Then she turned on both of us. "You can both go to the devil!" she stormed. "Don't you know I may never see him again?"

Her feeling was so strong that Dandré and I kept silent. She came to the boat.

She looked over my stateroom on the *Leviathan* minutely,

made sure that the bed was soft, that I was in a part of the ship where I would not feel the vibration too much.

She spoke to the purser. "Take good care of my friend Hurokchik," she admonished him.

She gave me detailed advice on getting enough sleep, on eating the right foods, on taking exercise on deck.

Then we said goodbye.

She had been right, of course, in her intuition. I never saw her again.

The first news came in a cable to the New York newspapers datelined The Hague, January 20th, and was headed

PAVLOVA MUFFS FIRST DATE IN 30 YEARS.

"Pavlova arrived here on Saturday, Jan. 17th, from Paris on her final world tour. On her arrival she was suffering from a cold contracted when she was in a train wreck coming up from the Riviera . . ."

Her death was tragically unnecessary. To the eye she was still beautiful, and her flesh fitted her slender bones with the perfection of a girl of twenty. But she was not a girl of twenty.

She should not have been making those killing tours, travelling in the bad winter months, sitting in ill-heated trains on long, jolting rides, suffering fatigue, courting illness.

When she was touring America with me she was at her peak. She had to keep her company occupied most of the year, she had to finance new ballets for the repertoire, provide herself with the best partners; her expenses were high, but her earnings were correspondingly high.

Nor had she squandered her money. She had lived modestly always. No lavish hotel suites, but only a nice room; no costly furs or jewels. She had no need of expensive clothes; she had elegance in anything she chose to wear. Her entrance in a room full of people was a dramatic moment. The way she placed her feet on the floor when she sat was an art. She needed no adornment, and desired none.

She had not even the excuse of financial need for constant, grinding work. Otto H. Kahn managed her securities for her, and at her death there was close to a half-million dollars in the estate, between Europe and America.

Why then did she work until she died of it? I have my own theory, of course, as everyone who knew her had. I believe she could not live without working, because she had emptied her life of everything but work, and it was by then too late to turn back and taste the kind of living she had missed. In another world, under another system, she would have been cherished like a jewel. She would have worked perhaps a few months of the year, would have danced perhaps once or twice a week. She would have had time and leisure both for working and for living, for love and children and the exquisite art of being happy.

Chapter Three

MY MEETINGS WITH PAVLOVA

Philip J. S. Richardson

I FIRST met Anna Pavlova in 1913. It was a hot July afternoon and I was helping Mr. Sherwood Foster with the arrangements for the huge "Versailles Ball" to be held at the Albert Hall that night. The feature of this magnificent costume ball was the pageant which represented a reception at the Palace of Versailles by Louis XIV, the King of France, of the reigning sovereigns of the period and their Courts, and when all were gathered Madame Pavlova and some members of her company, then appearing at the Palace Theatre, were to dance. On that afternoon the last squares of the great dance floor had just been hammered into place, the processions, in which many famous people took part, had been rehearsed, Corelli-Windeatt, the leader of the orchestra, was just leaving the Hall, when Pavlova arrived, accompanied by Mr. Daniel Mayer, and it was my duty to receive her.

In those days Madame Pavlova spoke little English, but I well remember her expressions of surprise at the vastness of the floor on which she was to dance, and her perplexity as to whether she should face the mock King of France (who was to be impersonated by the Grand Duke of Mecklenburg-Strelitz), or Queen Mary of England, who was to occupy the Royal Box in person that night. Incidentally it was a question that had worried the Ball Committee for hours, but Pavlova quickly decided. For her first dance, a Glazounov Waltz, she would imagine she was on the stage and dance to Louis of France, but for the second, a Mozart minuet, she would turn round and dance to Queen Mary. Her company at the Ball that night consisted of herself, Novikov, four *danseurs* and four *danseuses*.

A few days afterwards I entered the stage door of the Palace Theatre in time to hear the closing bars of the *Automne Bacchanale*, and five minutes later I was talking to Madame Pavlova in her dressing-room. Although she cannot have left the theatre until half past twelve, I found her the following morning at Ivy House, her Hampstead home, ready at ten o'clock to take a class of more or less beginners for two hours.

There were eight or ten girls in the class. I should say the youngest was about nine and the eldest about thirteen. The ballroom was a very handsome room surrounded by a gallery from which the rooms on the first floor opened out. At one end were large mirrors and a few chairs, in one of which Madame sat when she was not showing how some step should be performed.

The walls were lined on three sides with numerous engravings and pictures, including many original designs by Leon Bakst for the ballet, and a most interesting "page" from a "Confession Book" signed by Marie Taglioni in December 1872. I noticed that that wonderful dancer's favourite novelist was Walter Scott, her favourite poet Alfred de Musset and among her favourite composers were Mendelssohn and Auber. Several engravings of Taglioni

With Volinine in

Autumn Leaves

Autumn Leaves. Pavlova as Chrysanthemum and Hitchens as the Wind

With Novikov in *Bacchanale*

were at hand, and Madame Pavlova told me that she thought she must have been one of the greatest dancers we have ever had.

She described the "Russian" School to me as a mixture of the technique of the Italian School with all that is best of the French, combined with the peculiar temperament of the Russians themselves. The English, she thought, were not sufficiently emotional to become great dancers, and as young dancers they were always trying to copy someone else instead of being themselves. "Do not," she said, "give slavish imitations of the great dancers. Don't do it as you have seen 'So-and-So' do it, but do it as you yourself would express it. Your interpretation may not be so fine as theirs, but it is better to express oneself even indifferently than to be a mere automaton." When the class was over I was shown her garden, her favourite flowers, her chickens and her famous swans, which, she said, were decidedly bad tempered.

After that time I saw Madame Pavlova on many occasions in London, in the Provinces and in Paris, and every time she plied me with questions about what was happening in the English dancing world. Long before she joined her company she was asking me about Ruth French, and Ninette de Valois and Harold Turner were other British dancers whose careers she followed with close attention.

It was in 1927 that she paid a flying visit to the City Hall at Manchester on the occasion of the "All for Dancing Exhibition" and watched the winners in the various solo events, particularly praising Kathleen Spense and Harold Turner, who were then both pupils of Mr. Alfred Haines. Some rather sharp criticisms on modern ballroom dancing had been recently put in an article signed by herself, and we all joked with her on the subject, begging her to come and have a Fox-trot. . . . "But," she said, when she saw Victor

Silvester and his wife demonstrating, "that is beautiful, that is not what I object to."

At times Madame could be very *difficile*. Along with Madame Genée, Miss Bedells, Mr. Edwin Evans (music) and Mr. North (décor), she came to the Scala Theatre one afternoon in 1925 to judge the *Dancing Times* Solo Competition, but obstinately refused to understand what it was all about, and kept asking "Do they want engagements?" in spite of her fellow judges' lengthy explanations.

Through her husband she wrote to me from America when the "Operatic Association" (now the Royal Academy of Dancing) was founded in December 1920, giving the new venture her very best wishes and expressing approval of the scheme, but though she attended the last "Sunshine Matinée" and applauded Paul Haakon with all the force her hand could muster, it was impossible to get her ever to be present at a "Dancers' Circle" Dinner.

Earlier in that year, during the course of an interview while at the Palace Theatre, she had insisted that if dancing were to survive in England in its highest form we must have a central controlling authority—for preference a National School. I pointed out to her the practical impossibility of founding a National School at that moment—unless someone would donate an enormous sum of money for that purpose. A National School presupposed a National Theatre, and that was impossible then. "It would not be so bad," said Madame, "if one could rely upon the teachers, but both in this country and in America, particularly in America, I have come across teachers who have no right to be permitted to teach. They not only fail to teach what is accurate, but in many cases they actually do their pupils grievous bodily harm by giving them exercises entirely unfitted for the age and physique of the child. We are not machines. Every child of eight or nine is not the same." Madame Pavlova was horrified when she heard that anyone who liked in this country could pose as a teacher of ballet, and she said with some feeling that many who did so were guilty of an offence little short of criminal.

Madame also said, "I see that some teachers say they themselves are pupils of So-and-So, giving the name of some well-known and trusted teacher. That, of course, is better than nothing, but unless they have been with that teacher for some considerable time it means little. Young teachers should not say they are pupils of So-and-So unless they have So-and-So's permission in writing, which they can show to anyone."

"But," continued Madame, "you have some good teachers in this country. Cannot they do something to put an end to bad teaching and make it impossible for others to set up as teachers unless they are properly qualified?"

Two of the most impressive moments I ever remember in the theatre in connection with the dance were linked with Anna Pavlova. The first was at the old Trocadero in Paris, a building now pulled down. This huge concert hall was packed from floor to ceiling with an audience of at least 4,000 people for a Pavlova evening, and after she had danced *Le Cygne* she was given the greatest tribute that a performer can receive—those three or four seconds of perfect and complete silence—silence in which the proverbial pin could have been heard had it dropped—before the tumultuous applause broke out. She danced *Le Cygne* three times that night.

The other occasion was at the Apollo Theatre, London, on Sunday, January 25th, 1931. The "Carmargo Society" was giving its second performance, and two days previously, after a very brief illness, Anna Pavlova had passed away in her sleep at The Hague. At this particular Carmargo performance we had just had Ninette de Valois' *Cephalus and Procris* and the audience was awaiting the second item on the programme when Constant Lambert, the conductor, turned round and announced "The orchestra will now play 'The Death of the Swan' in memory of Anna Pavlova." The curtain went up and disclosed an empty darkened stage draped in grey hangings with a spotlight playing on someone who was not there. The large audience rose to its feet and stood in silence while the tune which will for ever be associated with Anna Pavlova was played. It was an unforgettable moment.

After Pavlova's death, at the sale of her effects at Ivy House, I was able to purchase a jewel casket which had been specially designed and presented to Madame in 1913 by her seven pupils, June Tripp, Beatrice Griffiths, Grace Curnock, Beatrice Colinette, Aileen Bowerman, Mabel Warren and Muriel Stuart. I had this mounted on a plinth and presented it to the "Operatic Association" (now the Royal Academy of Dancing) for an annual Group Dancing Competition. This event, known as the Pavlova Casket Competition, was run for a number of years, and now the Casket has been passed on to the R.A.D. Production Club. When I examined the Casket I found in one of the drawers six little silver hearts, probably each to represent one of the donors. One of these was presented to the winner of the Casket each year until they were exhausted.

Chapter Four

WITH PAVLOVA AT IVY HOUSE

Muriel Stuart

This contributor, who is teaching ballet very successfully in the U.S.A., started training under Pavlova when she was eight years old. Later, in 1916, she became a soloist in the Pavlova company, a position she held for ten years before opening her own school of dancing in San Francisco in 1927.—Editor.

A NEWSPAPER announcement that Anna Pavlova wished to train a small group of children prompted my parents one day to take me to Ivy House. The memory of the day remains vividly in my mind.

We lived, mother, father and I, in South Norwood, quite a distance from Golders Green. Mother and I took the train to Victoria Station, a bus across London and the Underground to Golders Green. I remember that we walked up North End Road and found Ivy House situated on top of a hill. How lovely it looked, the driveway bordered by tall flowering shrubs, the lawn in back of the house sloping downhill to a lake.

I felt nervous approaching the large front door which stood open. Marjorie Ford, Madame Pavlova's secretary, greeted us and we were taken into a large sunny room to wait, and I to change into my dancing dress. There were many other children already dressed in tutus and wearing pink satin ballet shoes. I remember feeling very upset while changing into my white china silk tunic and the soft dancing shoes which children wore in those days for dancing school. Finally my name was called and I went into the studio, a very large square room with a balcony surrounding it. Seated at the far end of the room in front of huge mirrors sat Anna Pavlova on a white bench. She was dressed in white and resembled an ivory figurine, her black hair outlining her lovely face. She called me to her and told me not to be frightened.

"Dance for me any way you please," she said, "but listen to the music. My pianist will play something for you."

I remember trying to keep in time to a Waltz, and later to a Polka. After my poor effort she asked me to come and stand in front of her. She examined my physical structure and asked me to point my foot, then took my hand and sat me down beside her, putting me immediately at ease.

Several other children danced that morning. She watched each one carefully. All of us were told that we would be informed of Madame Pavlova's final decision. A short time later my parents received a letter from Daniel Mayer, Anna Pavlova's manager, informing them that I had been accepted as one of eight pupils she wished to train.

Our lessons began at ten o'clock every morning and often lasted until twelve o'clock. She would go down on her knees to place our feet in the correct positions and go over each exercise with us with great patience.

I am sure those elementary classes must have been very trying for her. If sometimes she grew the least bit impatient with us we would burst into tears; on such occasions, and there were many, Dandré would later console us, rewarding us with peaches and taking us into the garden to look at the swans.

Sometimes after class she would talk to us and tell us that to be a great artist technique was not enough. "If you are going to be an artist one day," she said to me, "you must be sensitive to everything and everybody. You must see, hear and feel. For instance, you are going home and you will sit in a bus or train; there will be many people for you to observe, some tired, some sad, perhaps a haughty woman. Looking at them, try to understand what it is that makes each one so different. Listen to what they say and learn from each one something."

Not once but many times over the years she demanded of us the utmost simplicity and could not bear to see the slightest affectation in manner or dress. She taught us to appreciate all forms of art, encouraged us to read good books and to listen to the best music. Repeatedly she admonished us not to criticise until we had come to understanding.

Her company often came to Ivy House to rehearse and sometimes we were allowed to watch them. Nearly all of them at this time were Russian or Polish. To us they seemed to be the most fascinating and beautiful creatures in the world: Novikov, Madame Pavlova's handsome partner, Stefa Paskowieczka and Stasia Kuhn, the two lovely solo dancers, Hilda Buick, a member of the company and personal friend of Anna Pavlova. A continuous Russian chatter could be heard from Dunia Marnia and Kouzma; they made all the costumes for Madame and lived at Ivy House as members of the family.

Ivy House was always the scene of great activity. Many artists, painters and sculptors were her friends and worked there. Madame herself as a hobby enjoyed working with clay and often asked one of her dancers to pose for her.

I have never known anyone beloved as much as she, both as an artist and a person. The devotion lavished upon her by her audiences was matched by the love of everyone who was associated with her: members of her company, her household, even total strangers who would wait to see her backstage after performances. Often she would stay in the theatre listening for hours in her dressing-room to the troubles of some poor elderly creature; young dancers sought her advice, enjoying her attention and seeking encouragement.

I am not a writer and it is not within my ability to say just what constituted the extraordinary power she exerted. There have been wonderful dancers since Anna Pavlova, some perhaps with more technical brilliance, but she was a great spiritual symbol.

Chapter Five

CHORUS

Appreciation by members of the Pavlova Company

BEFORE World War I, into a remote hill station of the North-West Frontier Province, British India, came the words "Anna Pavlova." They were heard, repeated rather haltingly at first, turning themselves with strange inflexions round the unfamiliar Sahibs' and Memsahibs' tongues. But there they were, being spoken more and more often, usually accompanied by superlatives. One day a small girl caught them—or did their magic catch her? She asked her mother "What is Anna Pavlova?" "A dancer," came the answer, "a Russian dancer. They say she is the greatest dancer in the world." Touched by the spell, from that moment the child found herself being drawn, slowly but irresistibly from the everyday world into the charmed circle of the dance, the centre of which was luminous with the enchantment of Pavlova.

What was this unique enchantment, disseminating itself so mysteriously in all likely and unlikely parts of the world, through practically every strata of human society? It had none of the present-day media such as radio or television through which to work. No deliberate press campaigns to "build up" a personality were launched, and yet the name seemed to be everywhere. Everyone had heard it. Everyone knew who she was. The extent of her influence will perhaps never be known. Even today it is helping to bring courage to a young would-be dancer lying immobilised for months upon a hospital bed. She lies avidly devouring such books or pictures of Pavlova as find their way to her bedside.

The large specialised ballet public of today did not exist in Pavlova's day, yet wherever she went crowds followed her and, hurtling along in torrents of enthusiasm, climbed upon each other's shoulders, ran after her trains, jumped on to the footboards, and waited patiently for hours in pouring rain to catch glimpses of her. Wherever she went she was acclaimed. Up to the present time no other artist of the dance has actually performed in so many places and under such astonishingly varied conditions. She brought her art into direct contact with all conceivable types of humanity, awakening multitudes to an awareness of beauty whose existence they had not dreamed of before seeing her dance.

Children would frequently insist that they, too, must dance, and parental opposition to such an unheard-of career would disappear on seeing Pavlova. Parents of the fortunate ones who eventually joined Pavlova's company were justly proud of their offspring and, incidentally, such was the good name of the company that some very young girls were allowed to travel with it unchaperoned all over the world.

Pavlova chose her dancers with great care, and then sought to arouse the artist in each of them. There were times when tears of anger and utter misery flowed freely; but in the transformation of young dancers into artists her major concern was to make them *feel*, if they did not do so already.

Technique, or mechanics, must always be concealed and the desired effect appear spontaneous and effortless. Rehearsals when she conducted them were a nightmare for some, an inspiration for others. Her own intense sensitivity reacted alarmingly when met by insensibility or lack of understanding. The rapidity of her mental processes was well-nigh impossible for ordinary mortals to follow, and her uncanny ability to sense those of others was epitomised in her classic remark "Answer me! don't talk!" which came out all in one breath at the end of a lively admonition to a member of her company.

The wonderful fluidity of her own movement was quite inimitable, yet she would expect her girls to emulate it, at least in a degree. Rehearsals of *Autumn Leaves* were always anticipated by them with some trepidation. In this ballet the free adaptation of plastic movement to fuse with basic classical technique was fraught with difficulties. It demanded complete control throughout, together with individual softness of arms and body, and a sensitivity to each other's movements so as to blend perfectly in concerted passages and sudden—very exactly arranged—static groups, the whole to appear as windswept leaves. Again and again, regardless of time or fatigue—her own or anyone else's—Madame would work on these "leaves," never desisting until the result came as near perfection as she considered it could be brought—or until the curtain rose.

Before every performance she would practise on the stage, in her make-up, often continuing in the wings after the first ballet had begun. Sometimes she would watch for a while from the wings, when the company almost instinctively pulled up its protesting muscles. She would disappear into her dressing-room shortly before she was due to make her entrance, reappearing in her costume, immaculate in every detail, and followed by her devoted attendant carrying the usual impedimenta of emergency make-up, pins, needles and scissors. Perhaps she would say a few words to the ballet master, M. Pianovski, or to one of the girls, telling her how her hair should be worn, or that the powder she was using was a wrong colour. These remarks were not always uncomplimentary, by any means, and were always helpful. Then, in the shadow of the wings, Pavlova would brace herself, cross herself, moisten her lips with the quick, nervous gesture, so familiar to all those around her, and go to meet her public.

How can future generations ever become aware of her greatness? All they can know must come through their own artistic intuition; words alone are impotent to bring her to mind. Vast numbers of photographs are available, good, bad, and indifferent, but at best they are static. Some very old and imperfect film shots exist which, incidentally, she herself did not approve or wish posterity to see. This is very understandable, as the impression they give is so far from being a true likeness of the living original.

The fascinating structure of the dance, as we see it today, is the outcome of inspired and devoted work of countless dancers through centuries. Their various influences have acted and reacted upon each other, all contributing to the whole in greater or lesser degree, and passing their knowledge and ideas directly to each other—dancer to dancer, teacher to pupil. Accurate dance notation is invaluable in its way, but it can never reproduce the essence or quality of a movement, which lies beyond the written, or even the spoken word, and which transforms mere execution—possibly excellent physical execution—into dance. Like her many illustrious predecessors, Pavlova's influence is now being perpetuated. Though its source may not be recognised its effect will undoubtedly be seen eventually, just where she would wish it to be—in some of the great dancers of the future.

Kathleen Crofton

To the matter-of-fact English members of her company Pavlova was never quite real. To us doubtless emotional girls she was an immortal, rather than a creature of flesh and blood. How then is it possible after a quarter of a century to write of her from the "human angle"? Nevertheless, Pavlova could be very human and occasionally pathetic, for in spite of the public adulation she enjoyed for nearly thirty years she was a lonely figure, and towards the end of her life often asked "Would it have been better if I had had a child?"

This unfulfilled wish explains many of Pavlova's actions. Her deep interest, for example, in infant welfare, her financial support of a Home for Russian Orphans in Paris and finally her unflagging interest in the younger members of her *corps de ballet*. This affection for "her girls," as she liked to call them, was one of Pavlova's most endearing qualities, and was fully reciprocated, although at times her zeal for their moral and physical welfare became rather irksome and many ruses were employed to escape her ever vigilant eye!

Abhorring idleness of any kind, Pavlova believed in exercising the mind as well as the feet, and during the long train journeys necessitated by the great distances between "one-night stands" in the United States, she enjoyed nothing more than to walk up and down the full length of the corridor trains glancing right and left to see what the members of her ballet were reading—and woe betide any girl if Pavlova found her absorbed in one of the more lurid magazines popular at this time. To circumvent this "overseeing" of their literary tastes the girls devised a plan that worked like a charm.

For reasons known only to herself, the *Saturday Evening Post* was on Pavlova's "approved" list. Fortunately, it was large in format so that it was easy to conceal between its capacious covers any one of the smaller romantic novels in which, at this time of their adolescence, her girls took such delight. Poor Madame! she never discovered the subterfuge, and smiled charmingly when she saw her ewe lambs reading the *Saturday Evening Post* with such deep concentration.

During Pavlova's lifetime and after much has been written about her difficult temperament, some of these criticisms are justifiable, but in fairness to her memory it must be borne in mind that an international "star" lives and works under conditions of severe mental stress. At all times, and under all conditions, the public pay to see them at their best and nothing less will suffice. Is it surprising then, that before an important London, Paris or New York season they are in a state of high nervous tension? Pavlova was no exception. Rehearsals prior to opening were a nightmare, and the actual performances hardly less tense. Fortunately the company as a whole remained unaffected, for the more sensible members realised that on the shoulders of this frail woman rested the full responsibility of presenting to an exacting audience a well-rehearsed ballet with herself as the "scintillating star."

Of her magnitude in the world of the dance Anna Pavlova was acutely conscious. This arose not from personal vanity, of which she had none, but from a sense of perfection. An illustration of this can be found in the following story.

After several months of arduous travelling the company arrived in Washington D.C. for a three-day engagement.

Through an oversight on the part of the ballet master no class or rehearsal had been called for the following morning. Taking advantage of this unexpected release from the ordinary routine the *corps de ballet* arrived at the theatre with only sufficient time to make-up and dress for the performance. Half-way through this somewhat sticky process they were startled to receive a peremptory command to go up on the stage at once. Hastily snatching up whatever came to hand first they hurried, mumbling and grumbling, upstairs. On stage—all set for the opening ballet—they saw Pianovski, the ballet master, fussing and fuming, and Pavlova looking—glacial. At her bidding the girls formed a straight line across the stage, and then she asked them, slowly, one by one "Have YOU practised today?" The answer in every instance was a sheepish "No!"

Followed a moment of agonised silence. Then Pavlova walked slowly to the centre of the stage and drawing herself up to her full height said "*I* am Anna Pavlova, *you* are my *corps de ballet. I* practise every day while *you* do nothing . . . we will have a lesson here and now!" "*But Madame*," remonstrated the ballet master, the conductor and Dandré, her husband, "the curtain is due to go up in ten minutes—listen, the audience are in their seats."

Pavlova neither heard nor wanted to hear, and the class commenced. All the fury of which she was capable went into that half-hour of exercises; it was one of the best lessons she ever gave. The audience, becoming restless, were stamping their feet in slow unison but this goaded Pavlova on to further efforts, and only when she considered the girls had been punished enough was permission given for them to go below.

Pavlova's personal needs for a great star were modest. She possessed magnificent furs and jewels, but they were mostly safely stowed away in bank vaults. Wherever she stayed the rooms she occupied were comfortable but never ostentatious or luxurious.

In clothes her taste was impeccable. For day wear she liked tailored suits and for the evening favoured gowns cut on classical lines—and how beautifully they became her. If she had an idiosyncracy perhaps it related to shoes. She had dozens of pairs including—yes—red shoes! Lucky indeed the possessor of diminutive feet in the company, for a few pairs of Madame's always became available as new ones were purchased and room had to be found in the large travelling trunks to house them.

Official receptions, dancing displays at which she was the honoured guest, and private meetings with V.I.P.s all intruded upon her "spare" time, so that she was never really free of the obligations that arose out of her world eminence. It was not an enviable life despite the excitement, honour and glory, of which she had more than her fill.

Rita Glynde

THE magnetism of Pavlova's personality was no doubt one of the many reasons why she was so acclaimed—she had only to appear on the stage and the public at once realised they were regarding a being possessing some rare quality which passed to them across the footlights.

Not only when she was on the stage was this magnetism noticeable—often without knowing that she was near, those who knew and loved her could sense her presence.

There were times when, perhaps not keeping up the high standard of work she required of them, some member of

La Danse

Some acti
pictures
Giselle tak
during a p
formance
Covent G
den in 19
Pavlova
partner h
is Novik

See also op
site page

As Giselle. A Paris photograph taken for Diaghilev's first season in Paris

Pavlova's company would make special efforts, since though remaining unseen Pavlova's presence had communicated itself and it was well known that her quick eye saw all.

A young ballet student went with her teacher, a friend of Pavlova, to a performance of the Diaghilev Ballet. Just before the interval the teacher told her pupil she had a "feeling" that Pavlova was in the theatre although she was presumed to be on her way home from a tour of the Far East. When the house lights went up and Pavlova was seen to be sitting with her husband Victor Dandré in the circle, although the student was greatly impressed she did not realise until much later when she herself was closely associated with the great dancer how this "feeling" that Pavlova was near could transmit itself.

Although her personality was so strong it was also flexible and she could change it to fit each role she danced, in fact she became the dance itself.

Many members of her company will tell how even during rehearsals they were moved to tears watching her going mad in the first act of *Giselle*—she was a young girl losing her reason. They were awed and overcome when she rose from the grave in the second act. This emotion was not unusual nor was it confined to one or two highly-strung temperaments. It happened repeatedly just as each time *Giselle* was performed everyone felt from the moment of arrival at the theatre for rehearsal that the atmosphere was tense and that "Madame" must not be approached for any reason whatsoever—her mood must not be disturbed.

Surprise visits to the dressing-rooms of the *corps de ballet* were not unknown and it was essential that "Madame" should find everything—dressing-places and costumes—in good order. Even though there might be need for haste in changing costumes and often make-up, undressing on the way from stage to dressing-room was not allowed. How many who were closely associated with Pavlova regret her example of work and discipline? However tired she might be, she never overlooked any chance, however small, of studying anything that might be of value to her art. She arranged that her company shared all the most impressive experiences and in many parts of the world; exhibitions of native and folk dancing were specially performed for them.

When it was decided that a deeper knowledge of these dances would be beneficial, the company received lessons from native teachers in these specialised movements.

Pavlova was anxious that every member of her company should learn something of the art, culture and customs of the countries to which they travelled with her and should they not take advantage of these opportunities, she would have many unpleasant things to say regarding the stupidity of those who did not wish to learn.

One such occasion arose in Italy towards the end of an arduous European tour. After six months of travel, classes, rehearsals and performances everyone was tired and for once, having a free afternoon, most members of the company thought it a chance to rest or relax in one way or another. Four or five of them were playing cards in the lounge of their hotel when Pavlova, who had been to see some of the art treasures and old buildings of the town, walked in. That anyone of intelligence could be neglecting an opportunity to do the same, was more than she could bear. She vividly expressed her feelings. Cars were ordered forthwith and she herself accompanied the miserable card players on a sight-seeing tour.

That evening at the theatre everyone else was called to the stage and each was asked how the afternoon had been spent. The majority said they had slept.

"How you can to sleep in such beautiful town?" she asked, "You must to see everything possible."

It was pointed out to her that the daily routine, with classes followed by rehearsals when there was no matinée and the evening spent entirely in the theatre, left little time for sight-seeing and, moreover, this could prove a big expense.

Pavlova accepted no excuses and at once gave orders that the daily class should start at 9 o'clock instead of 10 o'clock so that until the end of the tour in Italy, the company should have the afternoons free and she told them that provided she was given an account of all they had seen and the impressions gained, she would pay all expenses.

To have been associated with Pavlova is an unforgettable privilege and experience and apart from the opportunity of travel which her company enjoyed, they were better paid than any other ballet company of the day.

Always provided that their work and behaviour were satisfactory, members of her company stayed with her for many years.

She liked to think of her company as a happy and united family and shared the troubles and joys of each member, trying to give them pleasure whenever possible.

Most of the girls in her company were young. She was eternally young in spirit herself and loved young people and her personal interest in each and every member of her company, not only in their professional life but in their private affairs as well, was deep and sincere.

Many receptions in all parts of the world were given in honour of Pavlova and her entourage and in order to appear at her best on one of these occasions, a young member of the *corps de ballet* was tempted to buy a dress she could ill afford. No detail of appearance or behaviour was ever unnoticed by "Madame" and it was not long before she saw the girl's new dress. The same evening at the theatre, as it was Pavlova's habit to give to those who could wear them, ballet shoes she found unsuitable to wear herself, the young girl went to "Madame's" dressing-room to fetch the six pairs she had been promised. She was just leaving with the shoes when Pavlova entered and instead of the expected words of congratulation on her appearance at the afternoon's reception, Pavlova asked: "What have you there? What you take from my room?"

"The shoes you said I might have," replied the girl.

"But, I not wish you have shoes," she was told and feeling as though she had been caught in the act of stealing, the girl was overcome with confusion.

Pavlova knew this young dancer had need to save as much of her salary as possible and by refusing the usual gift of ballet shoes, she guessed the girl would want to know why she had done so.

When, at last, the girl had recovered enough from her embarrassment to enquire the reason, Pavlova asked her: "How much you pay for dress?" It was obvious the dress was expensive and when she was told its cost, she said: "Too much! Very nice dress but too much for you spend! How much you save this tour?"

The girl had saved a considerable sum and felt rightly pleased with her achievement. She was, however, not unduly surprised when Pavlova replied: "If you not buy dress you save more. If you can afford waste money, you not need me give you ballet shoes."

Crestfallen and unhappy the young dancer was leaving without the shoes and had reached the door when she felt an arm slipped round her shoulders and with a kiss on the forehead Pavlova gave her the shoes, explaining that since the girl was young and her wardrobe adequate for all occasions, she should be wiser and less easily tempted in future.

Without a superb technique, Pavlova could never have achieved the status of *prima ballerina* in the Russian Imperial Theatre nor could she have endured for so many years the endless and continuous demand on her physical powers which her long and strenuous tours imposed, but she believed that "feeling" and not technique made the artist. Unless a *pas* was danced with feeling she would not approve, however perfect its technical qualities. How often was she heard to say to members of her company: "Why you waste time practising always to stand on one leg for half of hour? You do this many things very good but you not 'feel' what you dance—until you 'feel' you never be artist, only good machine!"

Much of her own inspiration was drawn from nature—*The Swan*, *Californian Poppy*, *Dragonfly* and *Autumn Leaves* were examples of this love and study of natural beauty. In her own character there was something of a natural simplicity—child-like and unspoiled.

She was seldom satisfied with her own performances and on one of these rare occasions, while the lowered curtains muffled the sound of the wildly enthusiastic applause of the Covent Garden audience, Pavlova rushed from the stage and asked one of the stage-hands if he had noticed how she had danced that night.

"Tonight I really dance good," she said, like a small child who, after performing some unusual feat, might say to its parents: "Did you see how clever I was to do that?" So, with the same child-like attitude, Pavlova wished that her dancing that night had been seen by everybody and that it had pleased them as much as it had pleased her—a moving gesture from so great an artist, acclaimed as she was, wherever and whenever she danced.

Perhaps because of this simplicity of spirit she was able to show the ordinary simple people of the world an art they could understand and perhaps because her dancing was understood and admired by the masses to whom she introduced the art of ballet, the influence and inspiration of Pavlova has been great and lasting.

Sylvia Kirkwhite

ANNA PAVLOVA, the greatest dancer of the century.

Many books have been written about Anna Pavlova, and in every one of them has been stressed the particular quality of her dancing—the indefinable yet unmistakable spiritual nature of her art—which never failed to strike her audience.

Her utter self-dedication to her art and her belief in the divine inspiration shone like a beacon through all her work and was the keynote of her outstanding ability. It was this unique quality which enabled her to convey to audiences composed of people in many walks of life, the sense of uplift which helped them, perhaps for the first time in their lives, to realise what a wonderful thing culture allied to true beauty could be, the very antithesis of the present trend of ugliness, coarseness and vulgarity which, unfortunately, has been known to invade even the Dance.

Her remarkable intuition enabled her to portray with penetrating exactitude the infinite variety of human character from the sublime even to the sordid. Moreover, this subtle quality of identification with the chosen subject helped her to express in a unique manner even the very life and feelings of birds, insects, and flowers . . .

How many people knew the real Anna Pavlova.

I would like to quote here the words of my friend Srimati Rukmini Devi:

> Anna Pavlova was certainly one of the most beautiful and inspiring artists I have ever seen. We believe in India that art is the language of the Devas, the Angels and Gods. If there was anyone who positively proved this theory and showed to the world the high worth of Art, Anna Pavlova was that one.
>
> Anna Pavlova was the exemplification of the Indian conception of the dance of Siva and the sublimation of the body so that dance becomes the music of the body and the body is transcended till it is no more the physical but is only the vehicle of spiritual expression. When she appeared on the stage, she electrified the audience and it was impossible to look at anyone else. It is to her that I owe the inspiration to serve as an artist and to assist in the cultural revival of this country of mine.

One of Anna Pavlova's most striking characteristics was her ability to stimulate the thoughts of others so that she could discuss with some of them topics which were of a great depth and importance to her and which formed a part of her *vie intime*. To such questions as: What is true art? What constitutes a true artist? Is a genius born or can an artist become one? . . . Her answer was always "The genius is born—not made."

Now a legend, the value and greatness of her impact upon art and culture will linger on for all time.

Cleo Nordi

"You are all my children"—these were the words with which Pavlova concluded a conversation as to whether she should give up dancing and bring up a family, which was her great ambition, or continue with her work. For her it was impossible to do both, for she maintained that no true artist of the dance could combine two such personal roles at one and the same time, for one was bound to suffer for the other. And so, much to her regret the idea of a family had to be abandoned for more and more journeyings all over the world, not only to the big cities where the opera houses and theatres were filled every night with audiences awaiting anxiously to steep themselves in the wonders of her art but long and difficult journeys to some of the smallest towns if they were lucky enough to possess a theatre or even a large hall.

How well we came to realise the meaning of those words "You are all my children." For we were young and impressionable, and in fact some of us had not quite finished our schooling. Taken straight from the class-room, with no previous stage experience, those who were privileged to tour the world with Pavlova lived as one big family. Strict discipline had to be observed at all times. Good living and our health were never neglected. Hard work, long hours and few parties were the rule, as we often left after the evening performance on our special train which would take us hundreds of miles to the next port of call for a performance the following day.

In most cases at Christmas time we found ourselves in a large town or city where we stayed a week or more—this we felt sure was pre-arranged by Madame—and these were the times when we understood those few maternal and often repeated words.

In Montreal, for instance, Madame arranged a real Russian Christmas for us. After the performance, sleighs with three horses forming a *troika* were drawn up in front of the stage door to take us several miles out of the city up to the hotel where Madame was staying. A bright moon glistening upon the deep snow on the ground, gentle snowflakes falling and the jingle of the bells on the horses' trappings combined to make this the most wonderful mode of transport on a Christmas night. Arriving at the hotel, we found a feast awaiting us, and then the most beautiful Christmas tree one could wish to see, superbly decorated and hung with parcels, with a magnificent gift for everyone in the company: leather travelling clocks, handbags, photograph frames, cameras, and workbaskets for those who sat idle for hours on end in the trains! Madame did indeed know how to bring up her "children."

One year, on our way to South Africa, we were all quite sure there could be no Christmas festivities as we were on board ship; only a few days more on the hard hot decks with little scope for practice, then Cape Town at the hottest time of the year and our opening performance the evening we arrived. But we were quite wrong. On Christmas day we were told that Madame Pavlova wished to see the entire company in the dining-room after dinner. At the stated time we all mustered on the stairs before the dining-room door which was locked. At a given moment the doors were opened to reveal the room in darkness save for the fairy lights hanging on a huge Christmas tree at the far end. Not one of us knew how or when that large tree was brought on board or transferred from the hold to the dining-room, decorated and hung with parcels by Madame, who was as excited as we were.

As mentioned earlier, our tours took us to all corners of the globe, to places where ballet had never been seen before. Therefore it can readily be seen what a great pioneer Pavlova was in taking ballet to the people—which was not so easy in those days as it might be now with today's means of transport—to pearl fishers in the far north of Australia, mining towns in the United States of America and of course in England, diamond and gold miners in Africa. In Townsville, a very small town in Queensland, Australia, not far from the Barrier Reef, having been told the "theatre" was small it was not long before Pavlova was on the spot directing operations, or rather giving instructions for almost a new stage to be built as the existing one was in such a bad state of repair.

It was just as well we took our own stage carpenter and electrician with us, for they had their work cut out to have everything in good working order by the time the performance was due to start. They were most loyal, and loved and respected Madame as indeed everyone did who worked for her or knew her. In spite of the fact that there was only one dressing-room for the whole company, Madame was as calm and serene as if she had been in a theatre of more normal size, but she was rather worried for the audience, who had to sit in deck chairs in the open.

This brings back memories of another time we danced out of doors. In Mexico City on Sunday afternoons we danced on a stage in the Bull Ring. At times this was rather disastrous because it usually rained each day at three o'clock. Even this did not seem to upset Pavlova very much, but she laughed with us one Sunday to see her well-beloved musical director, Theodore Stier, who was her sole conductor for fourteen years, conducting the overture while someone held an enormous umbrella over him.

In the theatre in Mexico the ovation Pavlova received when she danced the Mexican National Dances was quite remarkable. At the end of the dance sombreros were spun on to the stage from all parts of the house as a mark of appreciation and a great honour, for a sombrero is a treasured possession; its value became greatly enhanced after Pavlova had picked it up and spun it back to its owner.

Whichever country we visited Pavlova would always search out the best teachers in order to learn and have the company taught the dances of that country by experts. In this way she was sure of the authentic music, steps, tradition and atmosphere, and costumes. Thus, when these dances were well rehearsed and we returned to those countries their own dances were presented without fear of ridicule.

In Egypt we were given a day off from rehearsal in order to make a trip to the Sphinx and the Pyramids, in fact we spent a most interesting and enjoyable day in the desert. Our Dragoman was a particularly well educated and well read man and artistic too. He showed us far more than the average tourist sees. We paid him his fee for his camel men and proffered him a tip which he flatly refused to accept, so we gave him tickets for the ballet when we presented *Egyptian Ballet.* The following day he was round at our hotel to tell us how much he enjoyed the performance. He marvelled at the way Pavlova could look so like the frescoes on the walls of the old tombs, and how she could dance and move without shedding this illusion. Also the *corps de ballet* he felt had been trained to such perfection as to reproduce the ancient paintings and carvings. Of course there had never been a first-class ballet company of this kind in Cairo before and quite apart from our friend the Dragoman it made a deep and lasting impression on the audience in general. Our Dragoman insisted upon taking a little party of us to see the Pyramids by moonlight which enabled him to discuss with us Pavlova and art and the theatre—of which he was very fond—in all its aspects. Through various experiences of this kind we came to know and understand the real individual feelings of the people towards Pavlova. A few words here and there with many different types of onlookers gave us a far better conception of the attitude and reaction of the public to her art than any amount of applause from the auditorium.

Pavlova's insatiable quest for improvement is shown by the fact that she would ask the opinion of members of her company. For instance, one time in Holland a member was unable to work for a while owing to a cut on her face through a slight unforeseen accident on the stage. One night *La Fille Mal Gardée* was being presented. While Madame was practising before the performance she saw this particular girl on the stage, went up to her, put her arms round her shoulders and said "You go in front tonight, yes? I tink you go in front, you tell me how it is I dance, and you look my make-up, tell me all you tink." During the ballet this girl made mental notes about make-up, costume, dancing and work in general. Later round to Pavlova's dressing-room she went, feeling more than a little nervous because she somehow sensed that Madame wanted to be told something different from the usual praises, but how to be truthful without causing offence was rather perplexing. After all, for a mere member of the company to give judgment upon an artist of such fame and exquisite talent seemed more than a little presumptuous. However, Madame in the middle of a re-make-up for her next appearance turned to say "How it look to you, my dear? What you tink? Was bad?" No time now for thought; the questions had to be answered at once. Diplomacy mingled with the truth was the obvious solution. "Well, 'Madame,' I have seen you dance better." Here one or two little points were suggested. "Your make-up made you look about seventeen years old, which of course is quite correct for the part, but I think your eye-shadow was a little too heavy." Whereupon Madame at once said, "Ah! you tink I am bad. Never before have someone tell me I am bad." At this the poor girl felt her days in the company were numbered. She was about to try to rectify her criticisms when Madame's tone changed to gratitude and an explanation that she was so glad that at last someone had the courage to criticise her adversely, for as she so rightly said, "Everybody tell me, Madame you are wonderful, Madame you are marvellous. I know this is not truth because sometimes I not feel so good and I know I not dance so well. I can't see myself and so it is difficult to correct what is bad, but now you help, I am pleased." She then gave the girl a chocolate and a kiss.

Some of her criticisms of the members of the ballet were extremely apt. They could have been cruel if not said in just the right way with a twinkle in her eye and a laugh, but they sank deep and were never forgotten. To one girl who rather prided herself on her arms Madame once said, apparently *à propos* of nothing, "You know, my dear, there are three kinds of hotels. There is the first-class hotel, there is the second-class hotel and there is the boarding house. You have the boarding house arms." Another time when the girls were somewhat hilarious, only three simple words were needed to check the noise they were making with their chatter. Waiting to go on for *Chopiniana*, they were all talking at once just outside Pavlova's dressing-room which was almost on the stage. The door opened, out came Pavlova's head, and in a very sweet voice she said, "Who is listening?" Immediately there was dead silence. Everyone felt very foolish, but there was never cause for this little act to be repeated. There was no reprimand, no punishment, in fact it was never even referred to again. The simplicity of the discipline was such that Pavlova moulded and trained us all to her wishes. We had the deepest respect and love for her and were really all her children.

Joan van Wart

Chapter Six

A PARTNER IN PRAISE

Laurent Novikov

SOME of my most cherished and happy memories are those of Madame Anna Pavlova. We knew her in our family as *le coeur simple* and she was closer to us than anyone has ever been.

A good deal has been said and written about her ability and her influence on ballet. Undoubtedly she created a new era. From 1909 until her death her name dominated the whole world of ballet.

To me, the most remarkable date in the history of ballet coincided with her appearance abroad in 1909, at the Châtelet Theatre in Paris. Incidentally, the billing originally was to read "Imperial Ballet of Russia," but for some reason the organisers thought differently and it was changed.

"The Russian Ballet season in Paris might be entitled as a new era for the theatre of France, and indeed for all Western Europe," wrote Alexandre Bénois in his reminiscences.

Yes, it was new. It was new in repertoire, new in productions, new music, new ballet masters, and above all there was a group of faithful artistic collaborators.

But in essence it was the same academic tradition, the same

technique and construction of the performance, with the same splendid ingredients—the dancers of the Imperial Ballet of Russia. Yet what was presented then was only a fragment of the real Ballets Russes because of the very modest means at the disposal of this private enterprise.

Unfortunately the director and his collaborators in this private Ballets Russes overlooked the greatness of that talent that was Pavlova. They did not bother to create a special repertoire for her but strangely enough created for *un garçon d'un talent formidable*—Nijinsky—as everyone talked about him in Paris.

The attention was all on Nijinsky and nobody noticed Madame. Even the artist Serov's poster painting of Pavlova created more comment in the Press than did the model that posed for it!

Madame rebelled against an atmosphere that had grown within the company itself and after that first and only season, and in deep distress, she left the company. Years later, only, she made a few appearances with the company in some of the older ballets.

This step significantly affected Madame's whole career. Her vitality and enchantment required a freedom which she could never obtain in the Ballets Russes. Further, she had emancipated her mode of expression from academic and traditional routine and conventions some time before. So she founded her own company and for posterity this was the most happy decision of all. She found new audiences, many who had never dreamed that they would find in the dances of Madame so much emotional joy. "She made happiness by inducing others to forget the burdens of everyday life."

Madame's new company opened to unprecedented success. But it was the personal success of her great talent, for her productions were reduced to mediocrity by limited funds. But at least she could do what her heart desired.

In the naïve but sincere stories that her dances told, the entire psychology of her generous artistic soul was revealed. She could take the spectators where she wanted them to be; she could make them feel and see what she desired them to.

The magnitude of her personality was so great that her appearance in any dance was enough to create a tremendous impression on the public. And this to a certain extent explains why Madame's repertoire of ballets never presented any great creative problem. Besides, it was not her purpose to create sensations; she herself was the sensation, perhaps even without knowing it. She animated everything with her magic and sincerity.

Pavlova never adopted mere virtuosity of the dance as her goal, which was the dominant passion then among others in the ballet. She never deviated from her original purity and her ideas of romantic idealism. Thus she became the symbol of Ballet.

In my long experience with her as her partner I was forever impressed by the fact that she could interpret every shade of every facet of spiritual life and that, I feel, was the secret of her success.

But how much of this do we witness on the present ballet stage? Who besides Madame was more fully aware of the need for the plastic expression of music by the dance? Who can interpret with such fullness every variety of human expression? One would think that she had studied the art of a dramatic actress, but this was not so. She was the perfect virtuoso of her own perfect instrument!

Those of us who came from Moscow fully recognised her artistic trends from their early stages, and our celebrated painter Konstantin Korovin, after witnessing one of our

avlova and Algeranov in an oriental allet, with members of the company.

'nvitation to the Dance. Vladimirov nolding flowers), Varjinsky (on knee), Vilken, Borovansky, Arnaud, Hitchens, Surguev, Algeranov

Dressed for the first act of *Don Quixote*

appearances together in a *pas de deux* in Paris shortly before her tragic end, said "You were like a duet by two Stradivarius violins, playing enchanting melody with such poetical mastery that it cannot be duplicated in any other language."

Ballet is a "never never land" of make believe—to be enjoyed by those fortunate enough to be initiated. Let us never destroy that Shangri-La lest we disturb the immortal spirit that must be sleeping there.

Chapter Seven

PAVLOVA AND THE INDIAN DANCE

Ram Gopal

"WE were sailing through the Arabian Sea. It was evening and the most brilliant summer sunset radiated gold, red and purple. The sea had caught its magic ephemeral reflection and the mirrored power of those colours, in that quiet, with a low-hanging crescent moon, was so wonderful that I forgot I was on a ship ploughing through the Arabian Sea. Suddenly I was aware of another presence, for I heard a deep sigh escape from the slight figure standing a little way from me on the promenade deck. I turned to see more clearly, and there stood Anna Pavlova. She was gazing at the dipping sun, watching its burning crimson orb slowly touch the horizon. I turned to my left; there was nobody beside me. I turned to my right and she looked into my face. For a moment, which seemed like eternity, we seemed to become one in spirit with the great blaze of colour that Nature had set before us. . . ."

Those were the words of my friend, Diwan Chamanlall. I was enraptured by his description of that great experience, of his impressions of Anna Pavlova, of his friendship with her. Diwan Chamanlall and his beautiful wife Helen were two of the most erudite and discriminating of art connoisseurs in India, whose interests ranged from the Moghul and Rajput miniatures, of which they have a superb collection, to that of the Chola and Pallava bronzes. Their quest for and patronage of art had discovered and embraced, in the twenties, the rare talent of India's Amrita Shar Gill, the great painter who died so tragically in the early forties. How I had admired them both! I had learnt so much by listening to them talk of our Hindu heritage of the arts, of music, painting and sculpture. I had shown them and won them over to, the Hindu dance, and from those far-off days in the forties we had remained steadfast friends, ever seeking, ever learning, always searching for the "moment of revelation" that can be found in a picture, a jewel, sculpture, music, or a few lines of poetry. Here was Diwan Chamanlall, Diplomat, Ambassador of India to Turkey and a leading politician, talking to me in his dream house, that he and his wife had filled with the most exquisite works of art, perched high up on a hill outside Ankara. The date of that talk was 1949, during my tour of Turkey.

"Don't stop, Chaman," I pleaded. "Tell me more. What did she say, how tall was she, what did you think of her on those various occasions you saw her dancing? Tell me every single detail you can remember." There was a pause. "Ram, how can one describe Pavlova? How could *you*, a son of India and High Priest of our dances, describe the strange beauty of those temples in which you have so often danced? It is about as religious and monumental for me to describe Pavlova. Of course, I had seen her dance often, I had seen her *Dying Swan*, so many had; I had seen her frenzied *Giselle* in which the mad scene had made my skin tingle with goose-flesh. I had felt the cold breath of death as she rose in the second act, white, cold and dead, gradually warming to life till she literally floated around, hovering with her body like a humming bird beside her lover, only to be condemned to her grave at the break of dawn and to melt into the earth.

It was to me, a Hindu, a religious experience to see her dance. Her spirit and her expression reached out and touched me, carried me away, uplifted me and filled my eyes with tears, for in her art was great tragedy, a great veil of sorrow. In the dance she seemed to create an image of all classical music and drama and all the pathetic helplessness of the striving of the human spirit imprisoned within its mortal frame, seeking to burst forth and escape, as hers certainly did on those few occasions I can remember when she danced. I am afraid my attempt to describe her technical perfection in relation to the classical ballet is very poor. I know nothing about its technique and yet who cares about the scientific details and planning of the Taj Mahal when glimpsed by moonlight; it is unimportant. I have seen the great ballerinas of today, French, English and American, and I have no doubt they have attempted to turn faster, jump higher and balance according to the rigid standards required today but, much as I admire their industry, they seem to lack that spirit with which Pavlova imbued every movement. When Pavlova danced there were no strained neck muscles, no hurried movements, no conscious 'timing'; it was the whole effect of the spirit of her dances that enraptured and intoxicated one. It was indescribable and in the world of western ballet I have not seen her like." Chamanlall's voice had dropped to a whisper as if he was speaking of having seen some sacred Buddhist relic or, within his own mind, he was hearing and seeing some ancient religious music and Pavlova was dancing it within his heart, within memory's eye.

Bursting with excitement and encouraging him to go on talking, I asked: "Tell me, Chaman, was she interested in Indian dancing during her visit to India? What were our countrymen and art lovers able to show her of our great arts of dance, music, painting and sculpture?" Diwan Chamanlall came to earth, his face lost the look of dreamy reminiscence the memory of Pavlova had evoked, and he said: "Ram, you know so well the old, old story. When Pavlova visited India and danced in the big cities, Bombay, Calcutta and Delhi, not one Indian Raja or lover of Indian art was able to show her anything of the classical dance you and others have only recently revived in India today. She implored the wealthy and educated Indians to show her something of the mystic and exquisite Hindu dances she had always somehow known India possessed tucked away in her remote vastnesses, and yet the invariable reply Pavlova got was that the Temple Dance did not exist in India! Kathakali, Kathak, Bharata Natya (styles of Indian dancing), these were as hidden and unknown to the immortal Pavlova as they were, one is ashamed to say, to the wealthy and socialite Hindus who lavished every entertainment and hospitality they could on this great dancer during her two visits. The classic dance, she was told repeatedly, on both her tours to India was dead.

She was amazed and inspired to see the Taj Mahal by moonlight and told me often that it was the most beautiful thing she had ever seen on this earth. In fact she spent a whole night, till the early hours of the morning, watching the Taj Mahal by the light of a full moon until the first glow of dawn. She told me that somehow she seemed to have drunk so deeply of the spirit of India and the spirit of beauty, which she intuitively felt and understood, that she decided there and then to try and build an Indian ballet and express the essence and feeling that India's age-old monuments had inspired within her."

It is well known to lovers of the ballet that her subsequent visit to Ajanta and its thousands of years' old Buddhist frescoes and sculptures, had so inspired her that she created out of this in the twenties and danced a full-length ballet, *Ajanta Frescoes*, in London. With her unerring instinct and intuition, she had chosen Comalata Bannerjee, a gifted composer and one of the first young Bengali ladies of high-born family, to write the music, using the lyrical and enchanting Ragas and Raginis and Talas (time measures) of Hindu music for this Ajanta ballet, and also the Radha Krishna religious love theme. It was Comolata Bannerjee who introduced Uday Shankar to Pavlova as a suitable Sri Krishna to Pavlova's Radha. Every critic of the dance and those fortunate balletomanes who saw her Oriental ballets, *Radha and Krishna* and *Ajanta Frescoes*, as also *Hindu Wedding*, will remember how marvellously near to the "spirit" of India her dances were. She could not, would not call them authentic, but which Indian of the day could know what the word "authentic" meant in relation to the Hindu dance? Then, as now, the ignorance and confusion prevailing in the minds of a lot of self-styled Hindu critics is the rule rather than the exception.

Uday Shankar, that great dancer and pioneer of Hindu creative dancing, the late Menaka who revived interest in the Kathak dances of North India and her picturesque ballets, and Rukmini Devi who made it respectable for Brahmin girls today to dance "Dasi Attam," a dance of the temple courtesans; these three great artists who have done so much pioneering and spade-work for the younger generation of New Indian Dancers, were all alike inspired, bewitched, enraptured and inflamed to "do something" for the almost dead art of India. It was the magic quality in the art of Pavlova, both by her incomparable dancing on the stage and her electrifying talk and the nervous energy that she radiated off-stage to these three dancers from India, that inspired each of them with a determination to seek out, explore, create and revive what Pavlova disconsolately found and was told was dead or dying.

What dancer within living memory of the art of dance could be said to have so universally aroused, awakened and sown so many creative seeds and sparks, that were later brought to flame by these artists who had been "touched" or "graced" by the divine Yogini Pavlova? Shankar had the rare privilege of watching her dance, watching her rehearse, helping create a Hindu ballet for her. He toured with her, saw her nervous exhaustion and fatigue, saw her when she would drop exhausted and hysterical after rehearsals and performances in her dressing-room, saw her lightning temper flash and then melt into tears. He watched her intimately for as long as he danced with her in Europe and America. He learned how she created her roles; the beginning, middle and ending of them and her solos and duets, her lighting and sense of "theatre," and all the while he absorbed, drank and digested the great fire she had ignited within his own creative and artistic soul. He longed to do the same, somehow, in some way, for the Hindu dance.

One day his mind was made up. He would leave the great Pavlová and, come what may, he would dance, earn, starve if needs be, do anything, but somehow get back to India and SEARCH. This he did. After living within the glory and radiance she cast around her, he found New York, London and Paris rather cold and not very enthusiastic. He was alone and struggling to gain recognition by dancing, as items of entertainment, his creative impressions of themes of India. He persisted and even dressed up and danced as a Marwari girl, in headdress, short coat and skirt, and gained some engagements. Then he returned to India and, thanks to the inspiration and creative fire that Pavlova had aroused within him, went to Southern India, Malabar, and found, to his tremendous delight, the dynamic and fantastic all night, all-male dance spectacle we know today as the Kathakali dance dramas. He learnt under the great Guru or maestro Shankaran Namboodri, second only to the greatest living Guru today, Kunju Kurup, who is and has been for two decades the supreme actor-dancer in Kathakali. He took Madhavan, the brilliant young Kathakali dancer from the school of Vallathol and Mukumda Raja in Cheruthuruthi, near Trichur, in the heart of Malabar, and, using the mudras (hand cymbals) and kalasans (rhythmic patterns), created his great ballets.

Shankar went south to Malabar and found the spring from which he quenched his thirst. Menaka, or Leila Sokhey, a prominent socialite and wife of a distinguished Indian scientist in Bombay, who was head of the Haffkine Institute, went north. There, in Lucknow and Rajputana, she discovered the Kathak, surely one of the world's great solo dance styles, from which so much flamenco and Spanish dance seems to spring, brought by the gipsies and Moors, *via* Persia and the Middle East and during Muslim influence into Spain. One day researchers will establish the Kathak dance of the North as having been the original source from which so much in flamenco and Spanish dance derives today.

Menaka, what did she do? Like Shankar, she was a close personal friend of Pavlova, she taught her how to tie a sari and became a devoted and sincere worshipper at the shrine of the divine Anna. Anna had touched her too, graced her by look, gesture and speech; told her to search, to work,

With Novikov in *Amarilla*

Pavlova danced for some time with Uday Shankar and is seen here with that great Indian dancer in *Oriental Impressions*. Shankar arranged all Pavlova's Indian dances and ballets

Three of the many statuettes sculptured by Pavlova. Although they are not in themselves great works of art, they show a mastery by which the great dancer would undoubtedly have established a high reputation as a sculptress had she been able to devote enough time to what she practised at odd moments as a form of relaxation

In addition to her sculpture Pavlova also drew and painted. This pastel drawing amply displays her conception of flowing "lyrical" movement.

The first four panels of a "Bacchanale Frieze" of Pavlova by Malvina Hoffman, made in 1917. This frieze, which contains over thirty images of Pavlova, is in New York

With Victor Dandré in the
garden of Ivy House

During moments of relaxation, no matter where she was, Pavlova sought the advice of the many artists she numbered among her friends

create and dance. That was exactly what Menaka did. Before the last war she won a prize in Germany and got gold medals at dance conferences there and in other countries of Europe. Menaka constructed her "ballets" on Anna Pavlova's ideas of presenting a theatrical evening of the authentic mingled with the popular taste, both in India and the West. How successful Menaka was can be seen by her repeated successes in Europe and India. She used the Kathak technique for telling mythological Hindu legends and stories, in both her ballets and solo performances. To her must go the glory for reviving the beauty and awareness, both within and without India, of the grand style we know today as Kathak dancing.

So there we have the picture, on one side Shankar creating his exquisitely costumed and lyrical Siva-Parvati ballets, and other numerous themes using the elaborate Kathakali technique that suited his quiet power and finely sculptured body, and the late Menaka with her great physical beauty and perfection of face and form, working hard to learn as much as she could of the Kathak dance, and using that style for her creative and mythological ballets. Both were rewarded in India and elsewhere with phenomenal success. It is to be remembered that all three of the pioneers, Shankar, Menaka and Rukmini Devi were well into their thirties when they took up the study of the Hindu dance in India. So fired had they become and so intensely had the magic of Pavlova's personality and art imbued them that their one burning, unquenchable passion became dedicated to the revival of the Hindu dance.

After Shankar and Menaka, Rukmini Devi, a Brahmin lady of Madras, sought to revive and spiritualise the highly erotic and sexual dance "Dasi Attam" evolved by the Nattuvanars (dance masters) from the great Tanjore Temple dance drama known as the Bhagavata Mela Nataka, a dance drama performed exclusively by men in Soolamangalam. The "Dasi Attam" of the temple courtesans is a highly personal art form, filled with an emphasis on the Shringara (erotic love sentiment) rasa, ignoring the other nava rasas, nine sentiments that one sees in their full power and beauty in both the Bhagavata Mela Nataka and the Kathakali dance dramas. Rukmini Devi saw the greatest female dancer of Dasi Attam, Jeevaratnum of Pandanallur, at a music conference in the mid-thirties, in Madras, and was amazed at the strict adherence to tradition, the vast and obvious genius of Meenakshisundaran Pillai, the Cecchetti of Dasi Attam, and Bharata Natyam, and decided to learn all she could of this highly technical and exhausting solo dance from its most exacting teacher. With grim determination she set to work to follow the pattern and model of her inspirer and friend Pavlova. For six months she devoted her entire time to the great maestro from Pandanallur and in the beautiful grounds of Adyar, headquarters of Theosophy, she worked. At the end of that time she gave her first solo performance or Arengetral (dance début), and under the spreading branches of an enormous banyan tree a theatre had been built in the open air, and Rukmini Devi, at the height of her beauty and lissom charm and with her expressive and mobile face and eyes, danced her first recital of "Dasi Attam."

Gone was the crudeness associated with this nautch dance of the temple courtesans; instead one saw a beautiful woman dressed in white and gold silk, adorned with temple jewels of great antiquity. With flower-bedecked hair and her enormous eyes, she told the love stories of Krishna and Radha, Siva and Parvati. It was a sensation. Madras went wild and for years after that the name of Rukmini Devi dancing what was, till then, regarded by the majority as a vulgar and improper dance of the temple courtesans, but given a spiritual "twist" by this Brahmin lady in her mid-thirties, would fill theatres and halls to capacity. Rukmini Devi danced alone. I wondered when I first had the thrill of watching this unusual personality perform, why it was that she chose white, and then I thought, rightly, that she must have been inspired to wear this colour in homage to the white that the "Immortal Swan" hovering, swaying, dying in white, had worn. Instead of wearing that jewel, a blazing drop of blood that hung on the dying swan's breast, Rukmini wore a necklace of rubies, diamonds and emeralds; on her head, in traditional Dasi Attam fashion, she wore the "talai-saman" of the temple courtesans. When she danced her solo dance for two or more hours, one was entranced, enraptured and carried away by her beauty, personality and the grace with with which her Abhinaya (facial expression) was endowed. However, her purely rhythmic sequences in Thillana and Jathisvaram, and the Charanam portions of her elaborate Varnas were not as clear cut or equal to that of either Jeevaratnam, whom I had seen dancing in Mysore at a Durbar of the Maharaja there, or the younger Pandanallur Jayalaskhai, last of the traditional Devadasis that my great Guru and maestro Meenakshisundaram Pillai had trained in his remote and simple village home and dance school in Pandanallur some fifty miles from the town of Tanjore itself.

The western reader may find it strange that after only six months of training Rukmini dared give a recital that took a traditional dancer six years to perfect. The answer is simple. Rukmini Devi had assiduously studied Russian ballet technique and was an adept at barre work, also a rigid follower of the purest style of that great tradition. Louise Lightfoot, an Australian enthusiast of both ballet and the Hindu Natya, showed me many photographs of Rukmini taken in Australia; I was amazed to see pictures of the young Rukmini, looking rather like a double of Olga Spessivtseva, in tutu and ballet tights and slippers, *sur les pointes*, with the assumed faraway expression of the great Anna. Later I learnt and had affirmed from several theosophists that Rukmini had danced the *Dying Swan* all over the place at theosophic conventions of those times and, I am told, danced it very creditably. She worked hard at her Russian ballet technique and, thanks to what little she had learnt of this through her worshipping adoration of Pavlova, it enabled her to acquire in six months enough of the technique of "Dasi Attam" to give her own recitals with resounding success, all over Southern India and, later, all over the big cities of Northern India. If this met with less success it was mainly because of the Southern Indian singing which to Northern Indian audiences seems to jar and irritate.

There we have the vision of Rukmini Devi as I remember her in the early nineteen-forties, dancing like one in a trance in her "spiritualised" versions of the "padams" (love stories) of "Dasi Attam"; a picture in white georgette and gold or white and orange silk and decked in tasteful jewels of rare antiquity. Since then she has opened, and is doing service to the cause of art, dance, music and drama in a centre in Adyar, Madras. Were it not for her meeting and friendship with and adoration of the divine Pavlova, how many Brahmin girls today would dare to have danced an art considered at one time so degraded and corrupt as to be shunned by the Brahmin pundits, those who today extol it to the skies! Such are the heights and depths to which the goddess Terpsichore brings one; to fall and rise again. Certainly this is so in Southern India, where I was born and which enables me to speak from first-hand experience and knowledge of recent memory.

But for Pavlova! Yes, but for Pavlova, who knows but that there might never have been a revival of Hindu dancing, a revival that today in India has caught on like wildfire? The historical fact emerges that it was Pavlova who was the first to dance her version of a *Hindu Wedding* on a blacked-out stage at the Excelsior Theatre in Bombay in the twenties. With a gust of heavily incensed air, that clouded the stage and in utter darkness, the lights very gradually lit up the whole stage to reveal the divine Anna, seated, face covered and shimmering with brocades and silks and jewels. Here was a shy bride who at the conclusion of this *Hindu Wedding* of hers, got up and danced her joy at having married the one of her dreams and heart.

So to Pavlova again, who had a superb collection of everything she could gather, of the first lyrical, ethereal, romantic dancer of ballet, Taglioni, whom she idealised—Pavlova, emulating and equalling her with her own special powers of drama and tragedy, but using her as a model. Pavlova, with her magical powers over the audiences of London, New York and Paris, flying all over the world, drifting intangibly like a cloud, a wraith, flaming to life, panting and dying in an agony of spirit, or like a gust of autumn leaves, blown ruthlessly by the chilling winds of approaching Winter. What gods blessed this high priestess of the dance and with what powers? To engulf, to burn, to touch to life all those young souls the world over, with the fire of creation, who, in turn, have since suffered the agonies of taking to the life of a dancer, bearing and overcoming their lot; misery, sadness, loneliness, misunderstanding and precarious finances.

Untiring effort, sacrifice, tragedy and an unattainable goal of perfection made, in part, the legend that Anna Pavlova was in her lifetime. If there is one lesson all dancers (present-day ballerinas please note) have to learn, it is that, in addition to the rigid discipline of the classroom, the true dancer must absorb, assimilate, grow and experience at first hand a never-ending search for truth and God which, translated through the dance, spells beauty. This is only possible by constant awareness and absorption of life, in all its aspects, both the dark and the light, for it is through that ceaseless and eternal quest of the spirit of life, that a dancer, whether of Ballet, Spanish, Modern or Hindu, can radiate that flame and divinity which Pavlova personified.

Chapter Eight

PAGES OF MY LIFE

Anna Pavlova

Vivid are my earliest recollections, which take me back to the time when I was living in a little flat with my mother at Petrograd. I was the only child; and my father having died two years after my birth, we two were alone in the world.

My mother was a most pious woman. She taught me to cross myself and pray in front of the holy ikon in our sitting-room. The Blessed Virgin, whose sweet wistful eyes seemed to look kindly into mine, became a beloved friend. I used to hold conversations with her every morning and every evening, telling her all my infant woes, all my little joys and hopes.

We were poor—very poor indeed; and yet my mother would never fail to provide, on the occasion of feast days, a surprise for me, in the shape of some treat. For instance, at Easter, I would discover with glee some pretty toys enclosed in a gigantic egg. At Christmas we always had our Christmas tree, a little fir adorned with golden fruit shimmering with the reflected light of many little candles. And I can still remember my enthusiasm when one day (I was eight years old) I heard that we were to celebrate Christmas by going to see a performance at the Maryinsky Theatre.

I had never yet been to the theatre, and I plied my mother with questions in order to find out what kind of show it was that we were going to see. She replied by telling me the story of the Sleeping Beauty—a favourite of mine among all fairy tales, and one which she had already told me countless times.

When we started for the Maryinsky Theatre, the snow was brightly shining in the reflected light of street lamps and shop windows. Our sleigh was noiselessly speeding along the hard surface, and I felt unspeakably happy, seated beside my mother, her arm tenderly enclosing my waist. "You are going to enter fairyland," said she, as we were being whirled across the darkness towards the theatre, that mysterious unknown.

The First Call of the Vocation

The music of the *Sleeping Beauty* is by our great Tchaikovsky. As soon as the orchestra began to play, I became very grave and attentive, eagerly listening, moved for the first time in my life by the call of Beauty. But when the curtain rose, displaying the golden hall of a wonderful palace, I could not withhold a shout of delight. And I remember hiding my face in my hands when the old hag appeared on the stage in her car driven by rats.

In the second act a swarm of youths and maidens appeared, and danced a most delightful waltz.

"How would you like to dance thus?" asked my mother with a smile.

"Oh," I replied, "I should prefer to dance as the pretty lady does who plays the part of the Princess. One day I shall be the Princess, and dance upon the stage of this very theatre."

The Pavlova Casket. This specially designed jewel casket was presented to Anna Pavlova in 1913 by her seven regular pupils. After her death it was purchased at the sale of her effects by Philip J. S. Richardson, who presented it to the Association of Operatic Dancing (now the Royal Academy of Dancing) to be competed for annually by a group of not fewer than five or more than twelve performers in a *demi-caractère* ensemble or miniature ballet not to exceed five minutes in length. In a drawer in the casket were found six little silver hearts.

One of the most exclusive costumiers in Petrograd provided the costumes for Pavlova's first London season. The following year this costumier brought with her as her own assistant, Manya Charchevenikova. After that season Manya, as she was known to all who came into contact with her, stayed with the company as Pavlova's personal dresser. In this capacity she remained with her until the great dancer's death, gradually becoming an intimate and privileged friend.

Photo Roger Wood

A last meeting. Pavlova and Cecchetti, after a performance in Milan, 1928

My mother muttered that I was her silly little dear, and never suspected that I had just discovered the idea that was to guide me throughout my life.

When we left the theatre, I was living in a dream. During the journey home, I kept thinking of the day when I should make my first appearance on the stage, in the part of the Sleeping Beauty.

"Darling mother," I said as soon as we had reached home, "you will have me taught to dance, won't you?"

"Yes, certainly, my little Nura (that was her pet name for me), I shall," she replied, kissing me, and no doubt thinking of the joy she would experience in seeing me waltz at the time when, having reached a marriageable age, I should be taken out into society.

But it was not of society nor of ballrooms that I was dreaming. All my thoughts were centred on the ballet. That very night, I dreamed that I was a ballerina, and spent my whole life dancing, like a butterfly, to the sounds of Tchaikovsky's lovely music. I love to remember that night, which was to be the prime mover of my career, with all the joys and pains which it was to bring me.

The next morning I could speak of nought but of my great resolve. Then my mother began to understand that her daughter was a most earnest and determined little person.

"In order to become a dancer," she said, "you will have to leave your mother and become a pupil of the Ballet School. My little Nura would not like to forsake her mamma, would she? Most certainly not!"

"No," I replied, "I have no wish to leave you, Mamma dear. But if it is necessary for me to part with you in order to become a ballerina, I shall have to resign myself to it." And, kissing her, I begged her to secure my admission to the school.

She refused, and I began to weep. It was only a few days later, wondering at my firmness of purpose, that she complied with my desire, and took me to see the director of the school.

We were, as I said, extremely poor. And it was perhaps in the hope of providing for me at a time when she would no longer be with me, and when I should have to make my way alone and unassisted, that she decided upon that interview—no doubt a great sacrifice on her part.

"The regulations do not allow us to admit eight-year-old children," the director said. "Bring her back when she will have completed her tenth year."

And so I had two years to wait—two years during which I remained sad and dreamy, haunted as I was by the desire to become a ballerina as soon as possible.

I Enter the Ballet School

According to the custom of those who live in Petrograd, we used to spend our summers in the country, not far from town. It was always a pleasure for me to see our belongings, chairs and tables and beds and crockery and kitchen implements (not forgetting the big samovar) packed in a van and carried to the dacha, the wooden cottage no bigger than a doll's house. In Russia, when one is in the country, one is allowed to live according to one's fancy. And we elected to spend practically the whole of our days on our veranda. It is there we took our meals; and there my mother used to make me read Kyrlof's Fables aloud, or teach me to sew.

Bareheaded, and clad in an old cotton frock, I would often explore the woods close by the cottage. I enjoyed the mysterious aspect of the cloister-like alleys under the fir trees, all peopled with dancing butterflies. I sought out the most secluded spots, and would sit under a shady tree to build in the air the fragile castles of my dreams.

At times I wove myself a wreath of wild flowers, and imagined myself to be the Beauty asleep in her enchanted castle.

On my tenth birthday I told my mother that the time had come again to call on the director of the school. She looked very grave, but did as I had asked her.

I shall not attempt to describe my rapture when the director promised to secure my admittance to the school. Nevertheless, I shed tears when the day came upon which I had to take leave of my mother. She too wept. I did not understand the reason for her tears, as I understand it now. I was relinquishing the happy peaceful life of home, under the protection of the silver Virgin, and entering the very trying, intoxicating life of a widely different world, the world of art and of the stage. She realised that there could be henceforth no turning back, and that was why she felt sad; for, although one may fail to find happiness in theatrical life, one never wishes to give it up after having once tasted its fruits.

To enter the School of the Imperial Ballet is to enter a convent whence frivolity is banned, and where merciless discipline reigns.

Every morning at eight, the solemn tolling of a big bell would put an end to our sleep. We dressed under the stern eyes of a governess, whose duty it was to see that all hands were kept perfectly clean, all nails in good trim, and all teeth carefully washed. When we were ready, we went to prayers, which were sung by one of the older pupils in front of an ikon underneath which a tiny flickering lamp was burning like a little red star. At nine, breakfast—tea, bread and butter—was served, and immediately afterwards the dancing lesson began.

We were all gathered in a big room, very high and well lit. There was no furniture except a few benches, a piano, and enormous mirrors. The walls were decorated with portraits of Russia's sovereigns. After the small novices' lesson, the elder, more advanced pupils had their turn, and the beginners withdrew to another room, where they pursued their work.

At twelve the bell rang for lunch, after which we were taken out for a walk. Then more exercises until four o'clock, and then dinner. After dinner we enjoyed a period of leisure. Then came fencing lessons, music lessons, and from time to time rehearsals of dances which were to be performed on the stage of the Maryinsky Theatre. When we children had to appear in a ballet, we were taken to the theatre in great, well-closed cars. Supper used to be at eight, and an hour later we were sent to bed. On feast days were were taken to one of the Imperial Theatres: at times to the Theatre Michel, to see French plays performed by the French artists belonging to the Imperial company.

The most exciting days in our well-ordered life were those when the Emperor paid a visit to the school. In those times the imperial family used to mark their interest in the school by frequent visits. And then, to please the Empress, the children would perform a ballet on the school's little stage.

I can remember that one day, when I was a little girl, the Emperor Alexander and the Empress Maria, with other members of the imperial family, came to see one of those performances. At the end of the ballet we were allowed to go into the auditorium. The Czar took my little comrade, Stanislava Belinskaya, in his arms. He was so kind-hearted and unaffected, in all respects a true Russian! At that very instant I burst into tears. Naturally I was asked why I wept. And between two sobs I replied, with tears trickling fast down my cheeks: "I want the Emperor to take me into his arms too!" Grand Duke Vladimir, in order to comfort me, took me upon his knee. But I was not satisfied, and went on weeping and repeating, "I want the Emperor to kiss me!" The Grand Duke laughed heartily.

After the performance, the imperial family would come to the dining-room and have tea with us. We were not in the least embarrassed by their presence. The Emperor and Empress were so kind, so very much like a kind father and mother, that we were quite at ease with them, and altogether content.

Every Sunday my mother came to see me; and I used to spend all my holidays with her. During the summer we always lived in the country. We grew so fond of our little holiday cottage, that even now we have not the heart to give it up in favour of some more comfortable abode. And I am writing these pages upon a table on the veranda, amidst surroundings which I love because every feature reminds me of the days of my childhood.

I Become a Première Danseuse

I left the Ballet School at the age of sixteen; and shortly afterwards I was permitted to style myself *première danseuse*—which is an official title, exactly as that of *tchinovnik* in government offices. Later I was granted the title of ballerina, which only four other dancers of the present time have received.

After reading Taglioni's life, I conceived the notion of dancing in foreign countries—for the celebrated Italian used to appear everywhere. She danced at Paris, at London, and in Russia, where she is still remembered. A cast of her little foot is preserved at Petrograd.

One of the first exercises which the would-be dancer has

to perform is to stand on tiptoe. At first, the child can hardly remain in that position for more than a second: but methodical training gradually strengthens the muscles of her toes, so that after a time she is able to make a few steps—clumsily at first, and very much after the fashion of a tyro skater; then, in proportion as she acquires proficiency, the little dancer learns to walk on tiptoe as easily as a violinist performs a scale on his instrument.

After having mastered that first difficulty, the pupil has to get acquainted with steps of all kinds. The teacher performs a few steps; then half a dozen children imitate his movements as best they can for ten minutes, while the others watch. Then the little performers are allowed to rest, and others take their place. Apart from numerous, varied, and complicated steps which belong to the classical ballet, one has to learn a number of national and historical dances; the minuet, the mazurka, Hungarian, Italian, Spanish dances, and so forth.

As is the case in all branches of art, success depends in a very large measure upon individual initiative and exertion, and cannot be achieved except by dint of hard work. Even after having reached perfection, a ballerina may never indulge in idleness. If she wishes to preserve what she has acquired, she must practise her exercises every day, exactly as the pianist has to practise his scales. For the dancer must feel so perfectly at ease so far as technique is concerned, that when on the stage she need devote to it not a single thought, and may concentrate upon expression, upon the feelings which must give life to the dances she is performing.

Equal care must be devoted to acquiring the art of dancing with a partner, which is something quite special and apart. The ballerina must learn how to assume graceful postures in endless variety, to avoid conveying an impression of monotony which would induce weariness: for instance, when after each of her pirouettes her partner catches her in his arms. All this again calls for constant practice and no small variety of exercises.

At the School of the Imperial Ballet the history of the art of dancing is now included in the curriculum, and is one of the matters set for the yearly examinations. The art of making-up is taught with very special care and thoroughness; for a dancer is naturally expected to be capable of appearing at will as a Spanish maiden, or Chinese, or Greek, not to mention dozens of other types.

My first tour began with Riga, in 1907. That town, with its winding streets and its Gothic buildings, is German, not Russian. I arrived with a company, and we performed two ballets at the opera house.

The good Germans of Riga welcomed us so warmly that I felt encouraged to extend the scope of my tour. So from Riga we went to Helsingfors, Stockholm, Copenhagen, Prague and Berlin. Everywhere our dancing was hailed as the revelation of an art so far unknown.

At Stockholm, King Oscar attended our show every evening, which of course gratified me highly. Nevertheless I was deeply surprised when one day a chamberlain came to inform me that the King wished to see me at the palace. One of the royal carriages was sent for me, and I drove through the streets of the capital as if I were a real princess. The King received me in an immense room which I had already seen when visiting, as all tourists do, the royal palace. He made a little speech, very kind and charming, to thank me for the pleasure which my dancing had given him. He also granted me the emblem of the Swedish order "Litteris et Artibus." He told me that he liked the dances of southern Europe above all things; and that of all the dances that he had seen me perform, it was a Spanish one that he preferred.

I fully appreciated the Sovereign's most flattering graciousness; but I was even more deeply delighted by the spontaneous tribute of the big crowd that one night assembled, and paid me the compliment of escorting me from the theatre to the hotel.

There are people who refuse to believe that a dancer's life can be otherwise than frivolous. But in fact the dancer's profession is altogether incompatible with a frivolous mode of living. If a dancer, yielding to temptation, ceases to exercise over herself the strictest control, she will find it impossible to continue dancing. She must sacrifice herself to her art. Her reward will be the power to help those who come to see her to forget awhile the sadnesses and monotony of life.

That much I realised, for the first time, at Stockholm.

In the crowd which escorted me when I left the theatre, there were people of all stations: men and women belonging to the middle-class bourgeoisie, clerks and workmen, dressmakers' hands, shop assistants. They were all following my car, silently, and then remained standing in front of my hotel until I was told that they wished me to show myself on the balcony. As soon as they saw me, they greeted me with a stormy outburst of cheers which, coming after the deep protracted silence, sounded almost alarming. I bowed my head to them from time to time; and all of a sudden they started singing national tunes in my honour. I stood vainly seeking for a way of expressing my gratefulness to them. Then an idea struck me. I turned into my room, and came back with the wreaths and baskets of flowers which had been handed to me on the stage. But even after I had thrown roses and lilies and violets and lilacs to the crowd, they seemed loath to retire. I was deeply moved and quite embarrassed. I could not help asking my maid, "But what have I done to move them to so great an enthusiasm?"

"Madam," she replied, "you have made them happy by enabling them to forget for an hour the sadnesses of life."

I never forgot those words. By speaking thus, my maid, a simple Russian peasant girl, gave me a new goal for my art.

My Tour Through America

The following year I went with a Russian company to Leipzig, Prague, and Vienna. We were dancing Tchaikovsky's beautiful *The Swan Lake*. Later I joined Mr. Diaghilev's company, in order to show Paris the art of the Russian Ballet. Mr. Fokine, the ballet master, succeeded in pleasing the Parisians, who have so refined and so critical an understanding of art. He is a man of genius; and I am delighted that he should have succeeded at Covent Garden too.

Yet, the beauty of the scenes he combines, the splendours of the setting and costumes, the charm of the music, exercise so captivating and surprising an effect upon the public, that the dancer's individuality is lost sight of. Therefore Paris, whilst acquainted with the Russian Ballet in the form given to it abroad by Fokine's genius, does not know me as England and America do.

During the course of that season in Paris, I crossed the Channel in order to dance at a reception given by Lady Londesborough in honour of King Edward and Queen Alexandra. Their Majesties were graciously pleased to express their thanks for the pleasure which they had taken in my dances.

I returned to London in 1910, in order to appear at the Palace Theatre. Several friends had warned me that a first-class dancer belonging to the Imperial Ballet should not appear on the stage of a music hall. But I knew the London public and the London theatres so well, that not for one instant did I hesitate to sign a contract binding me to appear at the Palace. And I never had cause to regret having signed it.

The British public is most kind and sensitive. It has always been a great joy for me to find that British audiences evince a marked preference for the very dances I like best, and in which I give the utmost and best that is in me. I have the feeling now that perfect understanding exists between the British public and myself.

A tour to America, in the course of which I danced at the Metropolitan Opera, New York, followed by a London season. Naturally, I was delighted with the welcome I found in that country. The newspapers published portraits of me, essays on my art, interviews, and, to tell the whole truth, yarns of all kinds concerning my life, my tastes, my ideas. I have had many a good laugh reading those extraordinary fanciful articles, and discovering in them that I am the strangest and queerest person in the whole world. The American journalist may indeed be proud of his marvellous imagination.

After New York, our tour carried us through various states. It was a triumphal march, but an exceedingly fatiguing one. We lived in the special train which was taking us from one place to another across thousands of miles of country. Sometimes we would arrive at a certain spot with just time enough to go from the train to the theatre for the performance. Hardly did the performance end before we rushed posthaste back to the train, which whirled us away throughout the night (and perhaps the following day as well) towards some other town where a performance was due. It was desired that I should return to America the following year, and I longed to do so; but I lacked the physical energy to repeat so arduous a journey across the new continent. The ordeal is far too trying to the nerves.

We stayed at little towns in Canada: at Vancouver among other places. An incident which took place there, though trifling, amused me greatly; it illustrates the delightful courtesy of the Canadians.

After having danced at the theatre, I wished to go and have some supper at a restaurant. I found every table occupied, and not one seat vacant. Several people, having recognised me, offered their seats to me; and I was feeling so tired that in the end I accepted one. When I had finished my meal, a gentleman who was seated at another table stood up, and in an extemporised speech asked all present to drink my health.

His kind attention pleased me greatly. But I remember that my chief concern was for the old travelling suit which I was wearing—I am not ashamed to acknowledge as much: any woman would have felt the same under similar circumstances. But my old clothes did not stand me in bad stead: all responded to the invitation, and drained their glasses in my honour.

The next day, the incident was described in the newspapers. The Americans, eager not to be outdone in the matter of courtesy, paid me a similar compliment at Portland.

Art, The Sole Master of My Life

I have spoken so much about myself, that I think I may continue awhile, in order to reply to a question which is often made to me. In my opinion a true artist must devote herself wholly to her art. She has no right to lead the life that most women long for.

The wind rustles through the branches of the fir trees in

the forest opposite my veranda, the forest through which, as a child, I longed to rove. The stars shine in the evening gloom. I have come to the end of these few recollections. While writing them down, I began to realise more fully the purpose of my life and its unity. To tend, unfailingly, unflinchingly, towards a goal, is the secret of success. But success? What exactly is success? For me it is to be found not in applause, but in the satisfaction of feeling that one is realising one's ideal. When, a small child, I was rambling over there by the fir trees, I thought that success spelled happiness.

I was wrong. Happiness is like a butterfly which appears and delights us for one brief moment, but soon flits away.

Translated by Sebastian Voirol

Chapter Nine

LETTER TO A BALLET-LOVING NIECE

Arnold L. Haskell

Dearest Gisela,

No, I am not going to attempt to describe Pavlova to you or to answer your questions as to how she compares with your favourites, and for that matter, my favourites, of today. Only a poet would attempt the first and an accountant the second.

Yet, so vivid was her personality I can see every movement of every one of her dances in detail, and there are certain melodies that would seem trite to you and your friends but that to me carry the memory of great beauty past. I find them unbearably sad.

Thank goodness, I had ample opportunity of getting to know her work. My mother always booked for four or five nights of the week during a Pavlova season. What if I were a bit tired the next day or if my homework suffered! I had seen Pavlova and heard Caruso and Chaliapine. That was wealth, an investment for life.

Therefore when I met Pavlova after the 1914-18 war she was not in any sense a stranger. I knew her, I adored her and, of course, I was terrified. There is always something frightening about a really great stage personality, unlike those puppets of television who, like pet dogs, are called by their Christian names. I was introduced to her after a performance by Seraphime Astafieva, a fellow student of the great St. Petersburg school. I had not the time to stammer out the conventional phrases I had so carefully prepared when she assailed me with the alarming question—

"Are you on my side or Diaghilev's?"

Diaghilev had just given an interview in which he compared Pavlova unfavourably to Spessivtseva. It was unfair, even ridiculous, but quite clearly it hurt.

My reply must have made a good impression because she invited me round to Ivy House the very next day. There I was introduced to her husband Victor Dandré, who was to become my very good friend for a quarter of a century and who gave me the freedom of the house whenever she danced. And on some occasions when the house was full he stationed me unobtrusively in the wings. I have vivid memories of two such occasions. On the first she had just danced *The Dying Swan* to the usual thunderous applause. They shouted, they clapped, and they stamped; they would not let her go. When at last it had died down she passed me on her way to the dressing-room. She was furious. "How dare they applaud like that. I know I danced badly. It is no compliment to an artist. I shall lose all my standards, if people aren't more discriminating."

The other occasion, not so long before she died, was also after *The Swan*. The usual applause, some beautiful bouquets and a series of those wonderful bows each one of which was a dance. I was very close and I could see that this time she was pleased and felt that she had earned the reward. She looked like a schoolgirl who has received a prize, as if it were something unusual and unexpected. And then the curtain came down severing artist from audience. Suddenly I was looking at an old and very weary woman. I knew that I would not be seeing her many more times and that I must not miss a single opportunity.

I rarely saw her away from the theatre. She of course was busy and I was terrified of outstaying my welcome. Once however I did go to see her to tell her of a very remarkable young man named Frederick Ashton who was doing choreography for a group of pupils of Marie Rambert.

This may not seem daring to you but I can assure you that over twenty-five years ago it showed a certain amount of recklessness even to suggest that there was such a thing as an English choreographer, and almost a schoolboy at that. My enthusiasm must have lent me eloquence, for then and there she made a rendezvous to watch Ashton rehearsing at Madame Rambert's studio. We saw *Capriol Suite* and a ballet on the subject of Leda. She was enchanted, thanked me warmly for the introduction and said that Ashton must do something for her the very next season. There was to be no next season.

Just one final memory. I was talking to Fokine shortly after her death. He was criticising some of the modern dancers he had recently seen in America with their earthbound technique and their emphasis on the sordid. "It takes a genius to be gay, really gay. When I think of Pavlova it is not the classics, nor the sad and wistful evocations of ephemeral things, unique as they were, that I would give as an example of her genius, but *Christmas*. I cannot think of any other dancer who could even make it tolerable, let alone create something that was full of gaiety, the happiest thing ever seen in a theatre."

I have never forgotten that particular tribute.

Turn now to the photographs of Pavlova. They do I think show some quality. She posed magnificently, they are not merely records taken by the very latest in ultra rapid cameras.

Ever your loving Uncle,

Arnold L. Haskell

With one of the famous swans at Ivy House. To day some sceptics find the stories of Pavlova's friendship with these swans difficult to believe

A well-known dressing-room study

Chapter Ten

A CHOREOGRAPHER REMEMBERS

Michel Fokine

WONDERFUL was the art of Pavlova, great was the joy she gave to those who had the opportunity to see her on the stage.

Not only in momentary joys lies the importance of Pavlova's art, but in the great change of public opinion about the ballet which took place in the first quarter of our century.

She served as a marvellous proof, as a splendid example that the ballet could and should be an art in the highest sense of that word.

I knew Pavlova from childhood. We studied together at the Imperial Theatrical School of St. Petersburg. I remember her as a small girl in a blue uniform, with a white apron and a white cape, with tightly woven braids. She was spoken of as a "capable" and "a very attentive" child. But after graduation Pavlova began to stand out. She immediately took the position of a soloist. I danced with her *pas de deux* which were inserted specially for us in various ballets. Wherever possible we were included. These were typical *pas de deux* of the old ballet. We performed that which we could do best. Pavlova tried to do most pirouettes and I tried to show my elevation. There was absolutely no relation between the ballet and our dance added to it. There was very little connection with music. We began our adagio when the music started, and ended it when the music stopped. We went through our dance disregarding musical phrases and accents.

During such *pas de deux*, Pavlova would whisper to me, "Do not hurry, we still have plenty of music left," or she would say, "Faster, faster." At the end of such adagios we would invariably march forward to the centre of the stage, she on her toes, eyes fixed on the orchestra leader, I walking behind her with watchful eyes on her waist. While preparing hands to catch her, she would often tell me: "Don't forget to give me a push." To give a push means to assist in pirouettes imperceptibly, when a dancer makes one and one-half turns, the duty of her partner would be to give her an additional push so as to make two turns.

At this moment the orchestra would make the customary tremolo which the leader Mr. Drigo held while Pavlova was finding her balance. She would find it, spin, I would give her the promised assistance, Drigo would swing his baton, the final drum beat and we were both happy, and would take the final pose.

Many times we danced like that together, sharing excitement and bows. While performing and with the excitement in the presence of audience there was no doubt in my mind of anything we were doing. But when alone, I often thought, "What is it all about, does it mean anything?"

And it became plain to me that much was unnecessary and meant nothing. After rehearsals we would sit down to rest, I would express my ideas. Pavlova would agree with me, but I could see that my doubts made very little impression on her and after several of my speeches that what we were doing was not art she would reply that the audience likes it, and that if we would not make effective ending to our dances, we would not have any success.

Our argument usually terminated by her telling me, "Come on Micha, let's try it once again," and so we rehearsed. I felt her opposition to me in her very attitude towards the dance, the desire of success and applause.

From extra *pas de deux* we were promoted to perform ballets. We danced together *Paquita, Bayadère, Miracle Flute,* etc. To me, it seemed that matters became worse. We had to go through, in ballets of most varied types and periods, the same identical stereotyped scene. By pantomime I had to tell her the following: "I love you, and I want to kiss you." She would answer "No, I am so poor, and you are wealthy, you would desert me." I would have to answer: "I? Desert you? Never!" "Then swear" she would request. I would swear, lifting my hand up and would do that exactly in the same manner in all the ballets, it mattered not if I were a Hindu or an officer of the Napoleon army, or a mediaeval knight.

After performing such scenes, we would again have conversations and arguments, and again I felt that she did not fully agree with me.

But following the period of our *pas de deux*, and our mutual appearances in the old ballets, came the period of my experiments in the production of ballets.

I plainly realised that the time had come for a different treatment of pantomime and the dance. I also saw that in Pavlova I had found an ideal interpreter, that there was no discord, that she understood and fulfilled everything. One production followed another: *Grape-Vine, Eunice, Chopiniana, Egyptian Nights, Armida's Pavilion, Sylphides,* etc.

There were no more conversations of what the audience

liked, how to finish the adagio more sensationally, and there were no more attempts to sandwich in pirouettes.

Pavlova showed fullest co-operation, not only by eliminating effective tricks, but was willing to part with her personality for the sake of the role.

Before that time a ballerina, irrespective of the part she performed, was on the stage as she was in real life, in the same hair-style in which she entertained her friends at tea, in fact the very nature of the performance would bear a semblance to a party, with friends in loges, with the ballerina acknowledging their smiles.

The idea of creating an artistic image, the idea of transformation into a role, appeared only now. Only now appeared the unity of costume, make-up, dance, and pantomime. An entirely different approach to music demanded a serious consideration of each musical sentence and rhythmic detail.

Everything began to serve one purpose: the unity of the presentation. The ballerina became just one of the elements of the performance, and it was she who had to make the sacrifice. Pavlova did it wholeheartedly with inspiration.

I recall how I made her make-up. I gave her a sample of the colour to be used on the body evenly to appear like an Egyptian girl, in the ballet *Egyptian Nights*, then I painted on her face long eyebrows and made the eyes longer, and instead of cupid-bow lips, sharply outlined the contour of her mouth.

Soon very little of Pavlova remained, she became the Egyptian Tahor.

At that time, to me and even to Pavlova herself, it became clear that her power, her charm, was not in this or that technical trick, not in the final pirouette, but in her ability to create an artistic image.

I want to mention here about two compositions which played an important part in Pavlova's career as well as in my own.

In 1906 while producing the first *Chopiniana*, which was an orchestrated Chopin suite by Glazounov, I staged for Pavlova and my schoolmate Obuhov the C Sharp Minor Waltz which was specially orchestrated at our request by Glazounov in addition to the suite.

Sylphida, the winged hope, flies in a romantic garden lit by moonlight, pursued by a youth of the Chopin type.

This was a dance of the Taglioni style, that beautiful period of the ballet art when poetry was the main purpose of the dance, that forgotten period of the ballet when a dancer rose on her toes not from the desire to exhibit her steel-like toes, but with the minimum of contact with earth to create an illusion of a dance light, unrealistic, fantastic. This dance did not have a single pirouette, nor a single trick. But the poetic meaning of this duet in the air was so clear, so alluring! The public was captivated, and so was I. She created such a strong impression on me that I thought of a whole ballet in the same style, and at the next benefit performance produced for Pavlova *Les Sylphides*. Had Pavlova not performed so marvellously, so delightfully the Chopin waltz, I may never have ever created *Les Sylphides*.

Another of our works together was the *Dying Swan*. Everyone knows that this number was the most successful dance in Pavlova's career, everyone knows how marvellous she was in this number, but only few know what place this two-minute dance occupied in her heart.

I remember how that dance was created. Pavlova came to me one day and said: "The Choir of the Imperial Opera asked me to dance at their concert in the Nobleman's Hall, would you suggest some music?"

At that time I was a mandolin enthusiast and was just playing at home, to the piano accompaniment of my schoolmate, Saint-Saëns' *Swan*.

"What about Saint-Saëns' *Swan*?" I suggested. She immediately realised that a *Swan* would be most suitable for her. As I looked upon the thin brittle-like Pavlova, I thought—she is just made for the *Swan*.

"Compose this number for me," she said, to which I agreed and we arranged for a rehearsal.

The dance was composed in a few minutes. It was almost an improvisation. I danced in front of her, she directly behind me. Then she danced and I walked alongside of her, curving her arms and correcting details of poses.

Prior to this composition I was accused of bare-footed tendencies and of rejecting toe dancing in general. The *Dying Swan* was my answer to such criticism. This dance became the symbol of the New Russian Ballet. It was the combination of masterful technique with expressiveness. It was like a proof that the dance could and should satisfy not only the eye, but through the medium of the eye should penetrate into the soul. It is not hard to understand how I feel now, after Pavlova died, when I read that her very last words were directed to that dance.

Then came the Diaghilev enterprise, originating with Diaghilev's desire to present in Paris my ballets produced at the Imperial Theatre of St. Petersburg, and also from the desire to show Pavlova in Paris. Nijinsky and Diaghilev's interest in him and the desire to promote him came a little later.

But nevertheless, before the beginning of the enterprise Diaghilev announced Pavlova as a nearly equal partner to Nijinsky.

Such unfair estimation of Pavlova led to the fact that we

lost Pavlova from this great undertaking, and lost her forever.

She danced *Cleopatra* with me, and *Sylphides* with Nijinsky. She astounded Paris with her lightness and grace, the poetry of motion in the *Sylphides*, she was pathetic in dramatic scenes of *Cleopatra* . . . and left us.

I did not see her until 1913 when she invited me to produce ballets for her company. I staged the *Daughters of the Mountain Spirit* to the music of Spendiarov, and Liszt's *Prelude*.

In the second ballet, produced in the style of the Italian Renaissance, Pavlova had an exceptional success. In the audience were Richard Strauss and Arthur Nikich.

At that time I aroused no little criticism from the part of the musicians, still more from their heirs and relatives, for using symphonic music for ballets. I waited, anxious to know what these two musical authorities would say.

They both came on the stage expressing to Pavlova and me their enthusiasm. This was the last artistic joy I shared together with Anna Pavlova.

Reprinted from The Dance Magazine *of August* 1931

A SHORT CHRONOLOGY

1881 Born St. Petersburg 1881. This date seems to be the most likely although there has been some difference of opinion. At one time, and stated in the *Encyclopaedia Britannica*, 1885 was given in several chronologies. 1882 has also been stated. There is even less agreement on the actual date. Chujoy in *The Dance Encyclopaedia* gives it as January 3rd.

1891 Admitted to the Imperial School of Ballet, St. Petersburg. First teachers: Paul Guerdt, Christian Johannsen, Nicholas Legat, Eugenie Sokolova.

1899 Début at the Maryinsky Theatre, in the Pas des Aimées from *La Fille de Pharaon*.

1902 Promoted to second soloist.

1903 Promoted to first soloist.

1905 Promoted to ballerina. Begins to study under Cecchetti.

1906 Promoted to *prima ballerina.*

1907 Scandinavian tour with group of Russian dancers. Receives Swedish Order of Merit from King Oscar.

1908 Tour of Leipzig, Prague and Vienna. Adolph Bohm, Nicholas Legat and Egorova in company.

1909 Celebrates tenth anniversary at Maryinsky.

Appears in first Diaghilev season, Paris.

Tour of several European capitals with Mordkin.

Private performance in London, through an invitation from Lady Londesborough.

1910 First appearance in New York, at the Metropolitan Opera, with Mordkin.

First public appearance in London, at Palace Theatre, also with Mordkin.

1911 Long tour of U.S.A., and makes ast appearance with Diaghilev Company.

First full season with her own company at the Palace Theatre. At end of season Novikov succeeds Mordkin as her partner.

Appearance in Coronation Royal Command Performance of King George V and Queen Mary.

A snapshot taken about 1910

With "Duke"

A visit to the Sphinx, 1922

On tour in Holland, probably 1927

Outside the theatre, Bremen

On board with Laurent Novikov (left)
and Alexandre Volinine

Purchase of Ivy House, Golders Green, former home of the famous English landscape painter, J. W. M. Turner.

As guest artist gives performance of *La Bayadère* at the Maryinsky.

1912 First tour of the British Isles and second full season at the Palace Theatre.

1913 Third season at the Palace Theatre, after which company of English dancers is formed.

Tour of U.S.A. and tour of Germany.

1914 Engages Alexandre Volinine as partner when Novikov returns to Moscow for a rest, at doctor's orders. Tour of European capitals.

Last appearance in Russia.

A few London performances.

Tours U.S.A. and Canada. Spends all war years (1914–18) in North and South America.

1916 Stars in long feature film, *The Dumb Girl of Porticci. The Sleeping Beauty* has a six months' season at the Hippodrome, New York.

1918 In Mexico dances in open air before audiences of 25,000. In next eleven years travels with her company virtually throughout the world.

1920 Opens Home for Orphans for White Russian refugee children in Paris. Finances this home until her death.

1921 First tour of the Far East. Japan, China, the Philippines, Burma, India and Egypt. During the next few years there followed a succession of tours to many countries.

1930 Last tour of England, making final appearance at Golders Green on December 13th.

1931 Dies at The Hague, Holland, January 23rd. Cremated at Golders Green Crematorium.

INDEX

INDEX

Related Quality Paperback Books from Da Capo Press

The Ballerinas
From the Court of
Louis XIV to Pavlova
by Parmenia Migel

Dance is a Contact Sport
by Joseph H. Mazo

A Dictionary of Ballet Terms

"The clearest, simplest and least pretentious guide to the classic dance vocabulary that has ever been produced."
—Clive Barnes

by Leo Kersley and
Janet Sinclair

Steps in Time
by Fred Astaire
New Foreword by Ginger Rogers

Isadora Duncan
The Russian Years
by Ilya Ilyich Schneider
Foreword by
Sir Frederick Ashton

Nijinky, Pavlova, Duncan
Three Lives in Dance
Edited by Paul Magriel

Martha Graham
The Early Years
Edited by Merle Armitage

Diaghileff
His Artistic and Private Life
by Arnold Haskell with
Walter Nouvel

... available at your bookstore